CONTENTS #110
2015

NEW WELSH READER

'CASTOR & POLLUX', GEORGE POWELL COLLECTION

REGULARS

Editor 3
Rich Text: On Writing *Pigeon* Alys Conran 77

POETRY

Stallion Ford Nicky Arscott & Greg Koehler 8

ESSAYS

Bigotry and Virtue: George Powell & the Question of Legacy Harry Heuser 18
Somersault Coming of age memoir by Dai George 31
Violence and Transformation in Pascale Petit's Poetry Katrina Naomi 66

CREATIVE

Family Jem Poster 40
Mr Wolf Anna Lewis 51
Sicilian Driftwood Robert Minhinnick 59

New Welsh Reader
New Welsh Review Ltd
PO Box 170, Aberystwyth, SY23 1WZ
Telephone: 01970 628410
www.newwelshreview.com

Design: Ingleby Davies Design
Cover: 'I Hear Her Say', Nicky Arscott, detail from 'Stallion Ford', illustrated by Nicky Arscott.

Multimedia Assistants:
Emma Musty
Jess Rose

Principal Sponsor & Host:
Aberystwyth University

ISBN: 978-0-9930571-7-5
ISSN: 09542116

New Welsh Review Ltd publishes with the financial support of the Welsh Books Council and Aberystwyth University. New Welsh Review Ltd was established in 1988 by Academi (now Literature Wales) and the Association for Welsh Writing in English. We also work in partnership with Wales Literature Exchange.

Mae croeso ichi ohebu â'r golygydd yn Gymraeg.

Patron: Belinda Humfrey, Owen Sheers

CYNGOR LLYFRAU CYMRU
WELSH BOOKS COUNCIL

Noddir gan
Llywodraeth Cynulliad Cymru
Sponsored by
Welsh Assembly Government

PRIFYSGOL ABERYSTWYTH UNIVERSITY

Cyfnewidfa Lên Cymru
Wales Literature Exchange

WHAT'S THE TIME, MR WOLF?

GWEN DAVIES

WALES' ENDURING FLAIR FOR THE SHORT STORY IS GRADUALLY BEING recognized on an international stage, with our best writers in the form, including Cynan Jones, Robert Minhinnick, Rebecca F John, Francesca Rhydderch, Tessa Hadley, Tyler Keevil and Carys Davies having being recently recognized by prizes such as the EFG Sunday Times Private Bank Short Story Award, the BBC National Short Story Award, the Edge Hill Short Story Prize, the (American) Independent Publisher Book Awards and the Frank O'Connor International Short Story Award. The latter was awarded this autumn to Carys Davies' marvellous collection, *The Redemption of Galen Pike*, reviewed highly favourably in our spring edition (107).

Collections by promising authors of the form, Thomas Morris and Rebecca F John, were published between August and October by Faber and Parthian respectively. John was shortlisted for the Sunday Times award for a forthcoming story from her collection, *Clown's Shoes*, out in October. This book also featured in our audio review, broadcast on 1 November at newwelshreview.com/multimedia.php. Morris, meanwhile, appeared in late September alongside Davies at the Cork International Short Story Festival as well as joining the author with Keevil and Minhinnick in the widely praised and authoritative recent showcase, *New Welsh Short Fiction*, reviewed in our first *Review* supplement on 1 July at newwelshreview.com/list-review.php. Morris' debut, *We Don't Know What We're Doing* (Faber), meanwhile, was reviewed in our November *Review* supplement by Costa-winning poet, Jonathan Edwards.

In her review of *New Welsh Short Fiction* (edited by Francesca Rhydderch and Penny Thomas, and published by Seren), Vicky MacKenzie admires its celebration of the 'diversity... internationalism' and the 'sometimes downright bizarre' in contemporary fiction from Wales. MacKenzie emphasised that in this collection, 'form' is privileged above 'the hackneyed "slice of life" model' for short fiction or indeed any attempt to 'specially' represent contemporary Wales. The writers here, as MacKenzie notes, innovate through an epistolary tale, a film script with directions, and a dialogue with unnamed personae. This approach represents a return to form, turning its back on the subject- and issues-based bias of Dai Smith's Library of Wales anthologies, *Story*, Vol I and Vol II, published last summer. It reconnects with the modernism of short story veteran Rhys Davies, who was included by Katie Gramich in the *Encyclopedia of Literary Modernism*.

The latest anthology of winning entries of this year's Rhys Davies Short Story Competition, *Catch of the Day and Other Stories* (Accent), was reviewed at newwelshreview.com/list-review.php on 1 October. Dan Bradley quotes Davies' belief that a short story 'should contain' a 'tiny, concentrated explosion' and concludes that such 'miniature pyrotechnics', as Bradley coins them, characterise this collection, leading to structural predictability, 'snappy reveals and plot twists' rather than 'innovative writing'. In the prize's defence it might be questioned whether competition candidates pay any attention to the style of writers in whose name a prize is given. It is noteworthy, however, that commissioned and single-author short fiction collections, benefitting as they do from considered curation by editor or author, are currently getting better reviews than anthologies of open competitions.

Internationalism and diversity are also the trademark of the second collection reviewed at newwelshreview.com/list-review.php on the same date, this time dedicated to Japan's capital (and, hearteningly, presenting two translators from Wales, Dan Bradley and Jonathan Lloyd-Davies). Like Seren's collection, *The Book of Tokyo, A City in Short*

Fiction eschews national stereotypes. As reviewer Eluned Gramich puts it, 'any wistful narratives about cherry blossom are quickly dispensed with' and 'the ubiquitous tropes of bowing and chopsticks' avoided. Instead the 'black' mood of Rhys Davies' contemporary acolytes is favoured, alongside 'quasi-horror' and surreal touches such as a serial-killer satyr. The Japanese collection also shares with its Welsh counterparts an editorial policy, incidentally the USP of this magazine, of setting established writers (and translators in this case) alongside those that are emerging and previously unpublished. I wonder to what extent the Welsh collections share *Tokyo*'s conflicted preoccupation with what seems foreign, different or, even, more powerful (in the latter's case, 'The West')? But perhaps that would be an old-fashioned question that prioritises politics over style.

Our seventeen pieces of review and comment published on 1 October are exclusive to subscribers. If you missed them, look out for Duncan Bush on language, controversy and subsidy (*no*t Ruck revisited but hopefully stimulating response); John Barnie on the flaws of Alun Lewis, man and poet, as Lewis' unpublished novel and a second biography of him are published; Chris Moss on Robert Minhinnick's 'profoundly meditative' novel of life on the fringes, *Limestone Man*, and two reviews of books touching on (among a great number of other things) psychoanalytical approaches to Dylan Thomas. One of these is a rave review by Amy McCauley of John Goodby's *The Poetry of Dylan Thomas, Under the Spelling Wall* which she finds to be a thorough, original, vibrant and approachable work of scholarship which makes a tenacious and flawlessly executed case for reassessing Thomas as a worthy subject for serious literary criticism. The second aforementioned review is by Helen Pendry. This combines an assessment of the heavyweight *Liberating Dylan Thomas, Rescuing a Poet from Psycho-sexual Servitude*, with one of Philip Bounds' *Notes from the End of History, A Memoir of the Left in Wales*. In the former, she summaries Barfoot's rejection of Harold Bloom's analysis of Thomas' personality and her use instead of Kristeva and Lacan to reinterpret the poet's various infatuations, for example with material language as experienced through the senses, and with the body. Barfoot applies the same psychoanalytical filter to Thomas' apparent regression into a form of adolescence. This sensual obsession together with an apparent immaturity, Pendry quotes Barfoot as asserting, are 'not evidence of the infantilism of Thomas and his readers' but rather 'a form of "body-centredness" and "festival radicalism" that reclaims' the poet's notion of a 'maternal' source of creativity. Pendry's neat segue into her timely review of Bounds' leftist memoir claims, 'Both [books] suggest we damage our own souls... if we abandon the passions of adolescence in favour of becoming rigidly sensible adults.'

The pieces referred to above, along with a review of Nicky Arscott's pamphlet for Rack Press, *Soft Mutation*, and other articles, were published in the second of our subscriber-exclusive online supplements, *Review* 3, on 1 October. If you have not read or heard about any of these then you urgently need to contact Bronwen Williams on admin@newwelshreview.com to get your subscriber ID which you can use together with your own postcode, to vault our paywall. *Soft Mutation* shows an American influence on Arscott. This comes partly from her recent, Arts Council of Wales-supported research into emigration from her home patch of Llanbrynmair, Powys, to US states, particularly Tennessee. We are delighted to publish here in our winter edition of the *Reader*, what I think is an innovation for the magazine: a poetry comic, 'Stallion Ford', that is in a series with US poet Greg Koehler, and nails with tenderness and humour themes of longing, disinheritance and displacement. Migration, from, into and via Sicily, is also the subject of Robert Minhinnick's impressionistic and impassioned story, 'Sicilian Driftwood', while we are delighted to present newcomer Alys Conran's piece on writing her debut novel for Parthian, *Pigeon*, in a series of work commissioned from the author including a place in our winter poetry showcase video published on 1 November.

The rest of this issue is dedicated to our season's theme, 'Family', although this might easily have been 'The Domineering Father'. See our essay by Harry Heuser on George Powell of Nantcos' uneasy belonging to his family and his home town, which is expressed in his curious art collection and its long-delayed route to finding a home. And also one by Katrina Naomi on how the violence of Pascale Petit's conflicted relationship with her extremely abusive father becomes transformative in her poetry. Stories by Anna Lewis and Jem Poster contain the same patriarchal personality, although Poster's protagonist has a slow poison whereas Lewis' 'Mr Wolf' is more of a mythic, but no less dangerous, beast. The latter puts me in mind of Tony Bianchi's powerful exploration of what I take to be the effect of Autism Spectrum Disorder (ASD) on generations and within sexual relationships, *Dwy Farwolaeth Endaf Rowlands* (The Two Deaths of Endaf Rowlands). Bianchi excels across his fiction in the ASD-typical detached, hairtrigger-sensual, pattern-obsessed and micro-managing male protagonist, often living in the shadow of a domineering father with a similarly controlling nature. Our video interview with Bianchi, published on 1 November, explores how this came about, especially in his novel, *Harry Selwyn's Last Race* (Parthian). The video will also look at Bianchi's recurring motif of a witness' strangely inadequate response to the death of an intimate. *Dwy Farwolaeth* thoroughly deserved this summer's National Eisteddfod Prose Medal: never again will I hear the phrase '*Tyn dy specs*' (Take off your specs) or see Eric Morecambe wiggling his own glasses without turning to cold thoughts of domestic violence. So this edition's theme of the family's shady secrets returns. And yet in Bianchi's novel, while Endaf and Tomos share a dark father–son relationship, Tomos' mother and grandparents are positive characters, the family launderette is called Sunshine Cleaners and, despite Tomos' tussle at the border between solitary and lonely states, *Dwy Farwolaeth* ultimately brings its own brand of sunshine.

Part of this editorial first appeared on 1 October in *Review 3* at newwelshreview.com/list-review.php.

Stallion Ford

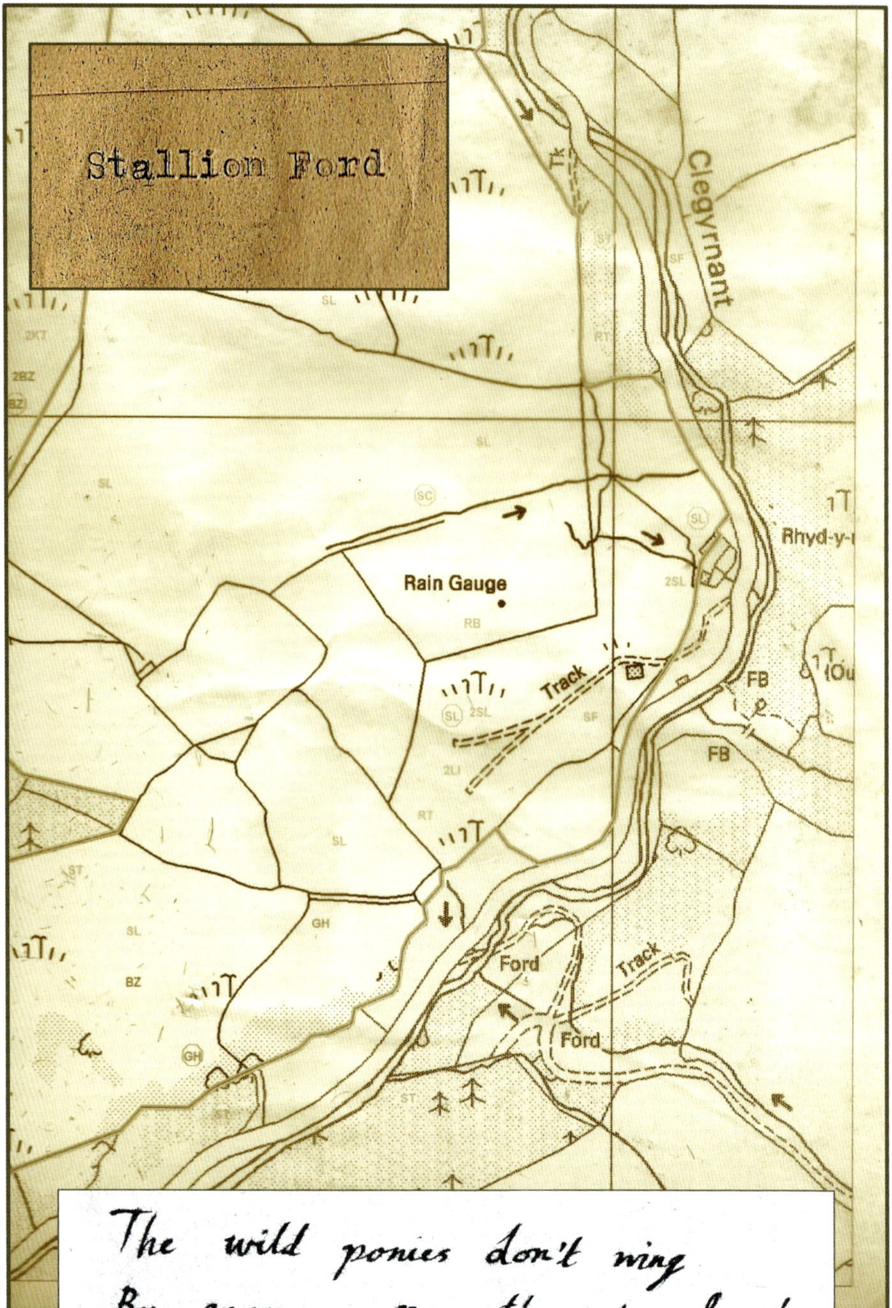

The wild ponies don't wing
By anymores now the pubs closed

an snuff grown in
The garden tastes
better
if bitter
nicotiana tabacum.

The child wanders in the garden
In the yard an I have a hear aye
I hear her say

I have a hard hiraeth.
My heart creaks.

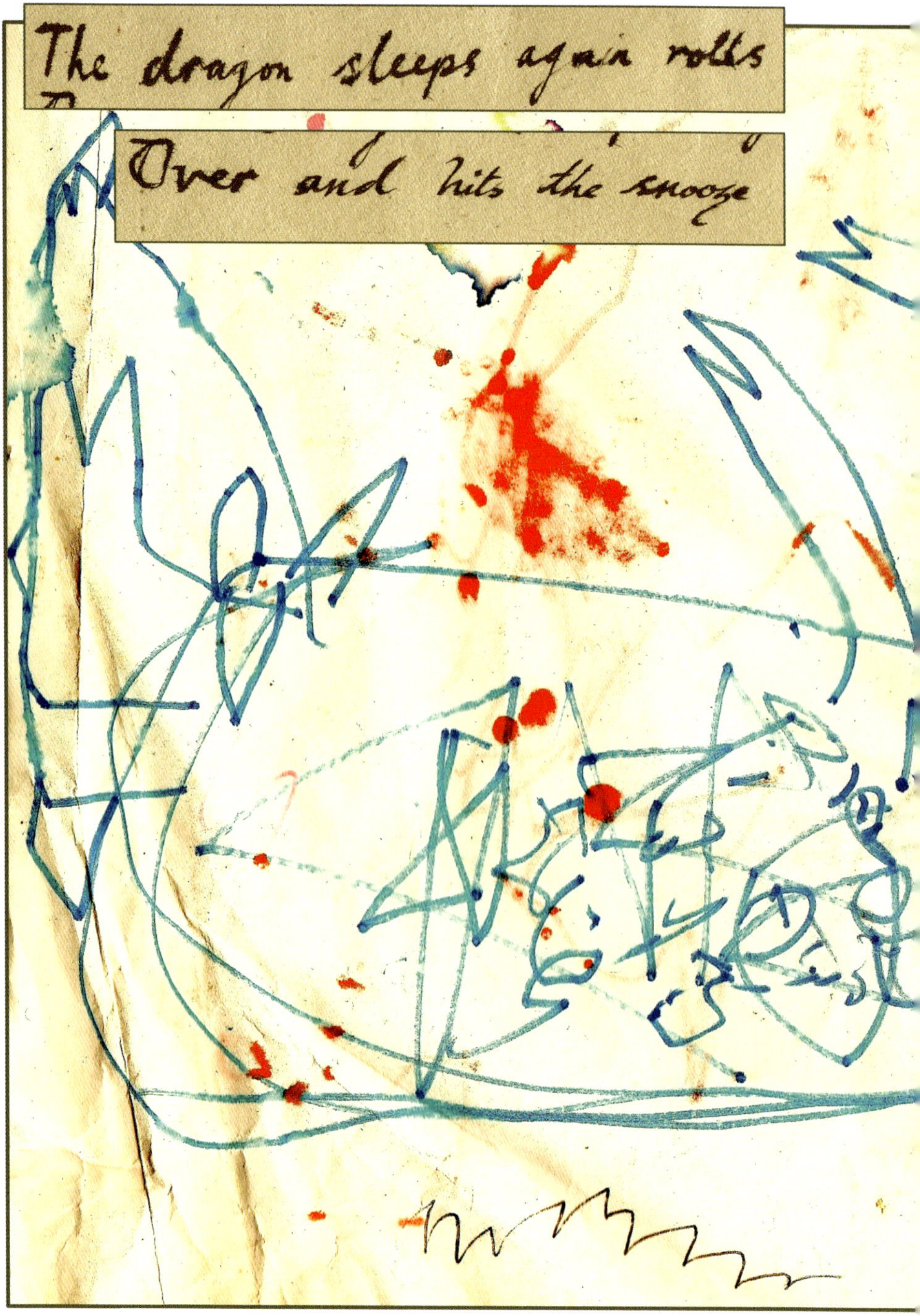
The dragon sleeps again rolls
Over and hits the snooze

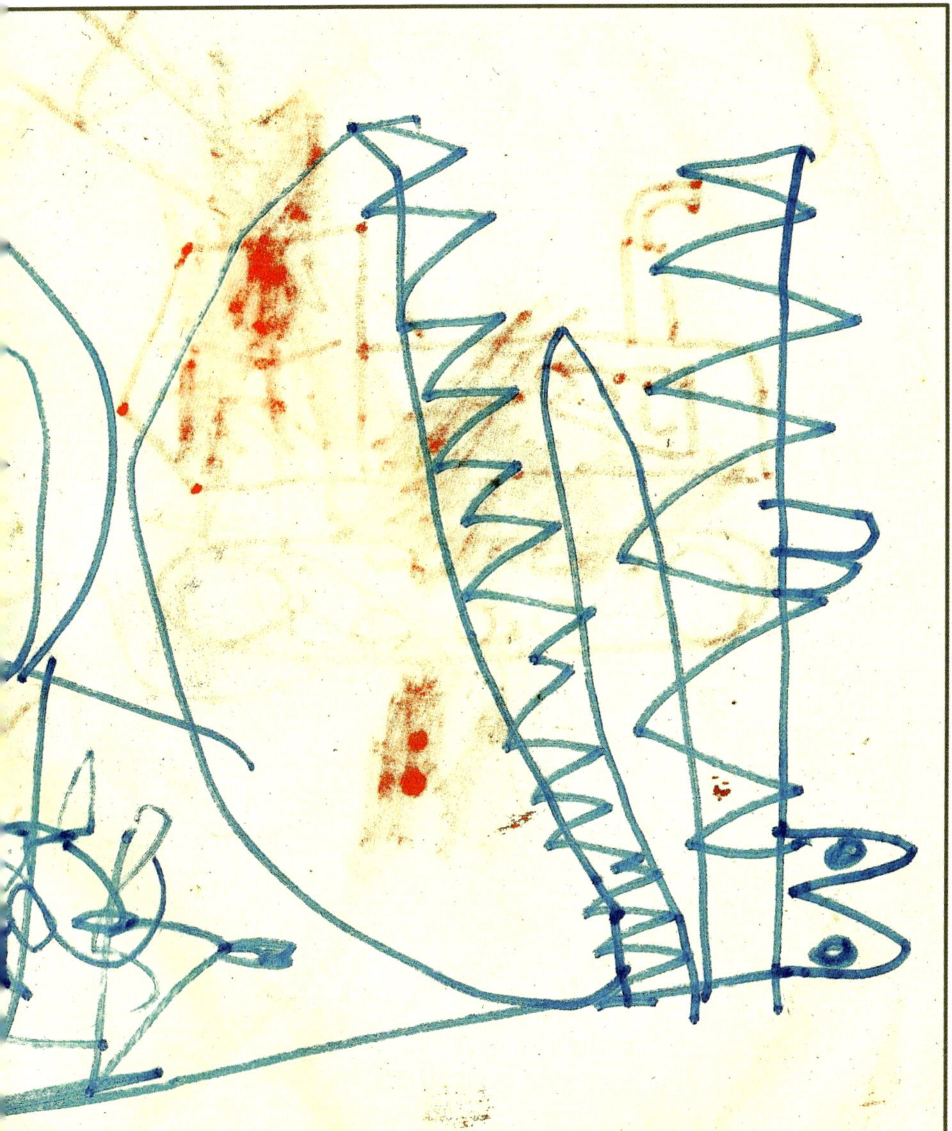

And belches and snores a sorry
Smoke.

Come back ponies come
Back pub. Come back Clegyr
And we'll take a dip and down
The bitter amber of Llanelli

The long bitter of my sullen spine.

STALLION FORD, A COLLABORATION OF IMAGERY AND POETRY IN COMIC-BOOK FORM BY

NICKY ARSCOTT AND **GREG KOEHLER**

NICKY: WE TOOK AS OUR STARTING POINT THE ATTEMPT BY SAMUEL Roberts of Llanbrynmair (preacher, pacifist, vehement anti-slavery campaigner) to set up a Welsh utopia, Brynfynnon, in the wildernesses of Tennessee in 1857. Not much is left of it now but piles of yellowing letters in uncatalogued boxes in the National Library of Wales. I spent many days poring through these in order to get a sense of what it must have been like to leave the place in which you had lived your whole life in order to settle an unknown territory.

The letters gave me a poignant insight into the problems faced by the Welsh in Tennessee, including the fact that the land had not been surveyed properly prior to purchase, leaving many of them with no option other than to join relatives or friends in cities in Pennsylvania or Ohio. For those few left behind at Brynfynnon, problems with Merino sheep, horses being poisoned by an unknown species of plant, and, finally, the outbreak of the American Civil War, left the settlers disheartened and vulnerable to violence and near-starvation when their farm was repeatedly ransacked by soldiers.

Greg and I met while studying creative writing at the University of Texas at Austin. A true contemporary Southern poet, Greg's poetry – full of history whilst colloquially very modern – made him the perfect voice to explore a retelling of some of the deep and rich stories that accompanied the phenomenon of US emigration from Llanbrynmair (the parish is reputed to have been the source of the most emigrants, per capita, to America of any in Wales). This is definitely just the tip of the iceberg:

there is so much material to mine that it feels as though we are just getting started down a long, dusty road.

As a visual artist and a poet I am always on the lookout for new ways to merge word and image. The poetry comic book seemed the most natural way to play with my own interpretation of Greg's poems. What we have tried to do with it is take the sense of hopeless longing that was so prevalent in those letters, and attempt to show how it runs through different people and places and periods of time: kernels of desire and failure that make these stories of emigration so human and alive.

GREG: While few Americans will know of Llanbrynmair and the large numbers of Welsh immigrants who left that village and came to the States, it is my hope that drawing attention to this fascinating story will be both entertaining and edifying as we shine a light on little-known stories from the Celtic diaspora.

As a visitor there in 2010, I was struck by the beauty of the low-slung mountains and the fields of grass roamed by grazing sheep. The place reminded me instantly of Appalachia, of the ancient hills and vales where thousands of Welsh immigrants made new homes in Tennessee and Ohio. The similarity of the landscapes, of the atmospheres of age and honour and remote dignity, are apparent in place, but also in the language and stories and hearts of the people who live there.

Nicky Arscott lives in Llanbrynmair, Powys. In 2014, she was the visual artist-in-residence at the Hay Festival. Her poetry pamphlet, *Soft Mutation*, was published in 2015 by Rack Press. nickyarscott.co.uk

Greg Koehler's poetry chapbook, *Tiny Ceremony*, is published by Mayonnaise Press (USA). He has written for the *Kenyon Review Blog* and *McSweeney's Internet Tendency*. He lives in Austin, Texas.

This project was made possible by a Research and Development Grant from the Arts Council of Wales.

BIGOTRY AND VIRTUE: GEORGE POWELL AND THE QUESTION OF LEGACY

HARRY HEUSER

When the collector, George Ernest John Powell (1842–82), decided to bequeath his artworks, books, antiquities and curios to what was then the University College of Wales in Aberystwyth, he wrote to Principal Thomas Charles Edwards saying that it was all he possessed of 'bigotry and virtue'. It is a curious turn of phrase to sum up a legacy – and a rather unlikely way of attracting an institution of higher education to it. The inverted commas were Powell's. The phrase was borrowed, they signal, and had been chosen advisedly. Might they be hinting at irony into the bargain? A cultured gentleman whose library contained numerous French volumes and whose summers were spent on the coast of Normandy – in a cottage he named Chaumière de Dolmancé after a character in a book by the Marquis de Sade, no less – Powell would probably have recognised 'bigotry and virtue' to be a corruption of *bijouterie* (trinkets) and *vertu* (articles of value and artistic merit). Yet the English meanings suited him as well. Not only did he expect academics to deliberate whether the objects he had amassed amounted to treasures or trinkets, he also realised that, by making his collection public, his own character would come under scrutiny.

George Powell (1865), by unknown, sent from Algiers to his friend, the artist, Johann Baptist Zwecker. Confronting expectations of what the son of a Welsh country squire should look like.

Bigotry. Virtue. There is a note of bitterness in those words – and for good reason. Some years before Powell approached Principal Edwards upon learning that the university had established a museum of its own, his ambition of making a difference in Aberystwyth by gifting his collection had been thwarted by the town council. Accepting though they were of what they acknowledged to be the potential nucleus of a museum and hence a cultural asset to the seaside resort, the council had failed to provide adequate rooms for its storage and display. Powell had given them an ultimatum and, after the deadline lapsed, he withdrew the offer. The debate about the gift and Powell's revocation of it were well documented in the local papers. Powell followed it all from his lodgings in London and chronicled it by pasting newspaper clippings into a leather-bound album. That album, too, would become part of his bequest, a tangible reminder to future generations of the injustice Powell felt he had suffered. As he expressed it with considerable fervour in his letter to the university, dated 4 March 1879, he had been '[r]epulsed by the more than coldness and indifference' with which his offer was received in what he described as the 'general Methodistic gloom' of his 'dear but benighted town'. Not that this is quite what happened, given that the council had succeeded in getting ratepayers to adopt the Public Libraries and Museums Act of 1855, a necessary step for making the building of a museum for Aberystwyth possible. Powell felt himself rebuffed all the same, and he may have wondered whether there was anything more to that perceived 'coldness'. Yet he could not bring himself to pursue the matter in person by returning to the place of his childhood and youth.

Opposite: High-shouldered vase (c1870s Japanese), glazed stoneware with design in thick enamel.
Overleaf: (L) 'Roman Youth' (1869), Simeon Solomon, watercolour; (R) 'Bound Slave' (mid-19th century French), bronze. Note the bound figure, the state of bondage and the theme of enslavement. A young black servant worked at Powell's cottage in Normandy. Swinburne and Powell exchanged notes on corporal punishment and may have frequented a brother catering for flagellation.

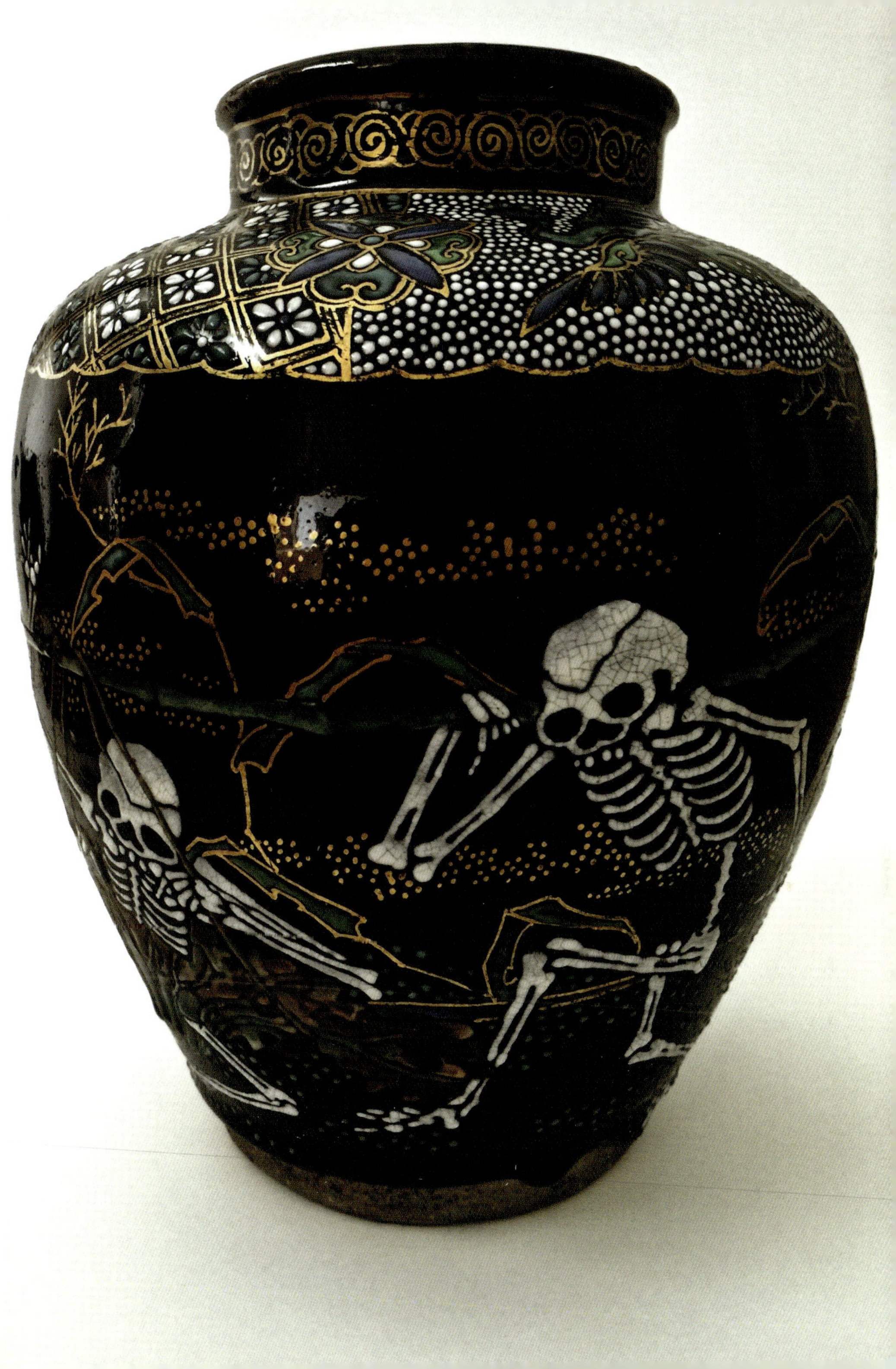

1869
ROME

In other words, his belongings were meant for a town in which he no longer felt he belonged.

As a gay, US-educated German expatriate now living in Wales, I am no stranger to crises of identity. And, for that reason, I have found myself drawn to George Powell of Nanteos, a marginalised 'Welshman' – English-born, Eton-schooled and Oxford-educated – whom one historian aptly called a 'misfit in the squirearchical society' of Wales. I have been speculating about Powell's life and longings in a chapter for the forthcoming anthology, *Queer Wales* and, together with my students at the School of Art at Aberystwyth University, recently curated *Queer Tastes*, an exhibition that speculated about Powell's life by examining the artworks and artefacts he bequeathed to us. Eclectic and seemingly unprincipled, the Powell bequest raises questions about identity and legacy that are likely to have crossed the mind of anyone whose life and work have been found wanting in national relevance, anyone who has ever experienced that queer feeling of being neither here nor there. Who did Powell think he was, leaving us a rock crystal casket that allegedly contained a splinter of Robert Schumann's coffin? What was it that attracted him to a series of forensic studies, executed in pen, ink and watercolour by a student of the painter Jacques-Louis David and intended to document the 'physical transformations undergone by cadavers rotting in the earth, in water, in toilets and in manure'? And how about those odd volumes that stood alongside the classics in his library: books on hallucinations, Greek love, insanity, suicide, witchcraft and animal magnetism?

The Powell bequest was hardly an assemblage of undisputed masterpieces, authentic crafts and authoritative tomes. Sure, it contained watercolour paintings by noted artists such as JMW Turner, etchings by John Hamilton Mortimer as well as drawings by Dante Gabriel Rossetti and Edward Burne-Jones. But what would academics – or the general public – make of a dried flower that Powell claimed to have plucked from composer Richard Wagner's garden at Bayreuth? What 'virtue' would gallery-goers find in a portrait of Powell's pet monkey, Nip? And what 'bigotry' might be incited locally by artworks and books that represent Icelandic legends instead of being representative of Welsh culture? Perhaps, all that Powell possessed of 'bigotry and virtue' was representative of nothing more – nor anything less – than the passion of a single individual who made a virtue of being different. Reading the bequest like a fragmented autobiography, it struck me that what Powell left to us was not so much an orderly, finite collection as a trail of objects that, inviting infinite questions, implore us to go in search of the man. The bequest was his – but that quest is ours to make.

The son of a squire residing in an ancestral mansion near Aberystwyth, Powell was determined to make a name for himself that stood for something other than a tradition of entitlement. His family home, Nanteos, had been an unhappy one. His younger sister died of tuberculosis in 1857. Three years later, when Powell was eighteen, his mother died from 'the breaking of a blood vessel'; accused of adultery, she had been separated from George's father, Colonel William Thomas Rowland Powell, who by then was partially paralysed and confined to a wheelchair. To the colonel, his heir had been a consummate disappointment. One writer, a granddaughter of a distant cousin of Powell's, described the father as 'bluff' and 'militaristic', a bigot who thought of his son as a 'feeble dreamer, damnedly artistic like his mother, and no good with a gun.' Instead of going hunting, the young man wrote poetry, which he had privately printed in Aberystwyth. Adopting the nom de guerre, 'Miölnir', the hammer of Thor, he seemed anxious to crush expectations; but proudly, or defiantly, he added 'Nant-Eos' to his pseudonym, so that there could be little doubt as to the identity of the writer or the conventions he was up against. When, in 1866, the colonel forbade his son from setting foot onto the estate, Powell vowed never to return to the place that, to him, was 'home' in all but a 'sentimental sense'.

Powell's correspondences, along with the legal documents that are now held in the Ceredigion Archives in Aberystwyth, allow us, to some extent, to patch together his story. It is his collection that makes Powell's self-fashioning palpable. His rejection and defiance are visualised in works like Richard Westall's watercolour painting, *Satan Summoning His Legions*, a Miltonic take on the fallen angel, or Étienne Barthélémy Garnier's pencil drawing of the superheroic Ajax who, once disgraced, would commit suicide rather than face his father. And then there are works like Simeon Solomon's *Love Dreaming by the Sea* or Johann Baptist Zwecker's fantasy of a boy on a dragonfly. These watercolour paintings, which were commissioned by Powell and executed to his specifications, luxuriate in the daydreams that Powell's father had dismissed as idle and fruitless.

A passionate, undisciplined college dropout, Powell cultivated this perceived idleness by becoming a dilettante. Living in London and France, and travelling to Russia, North Africa and Iceland, he adopted various guises and modes, be it as connoisseur of Western art or Eastern crafts, translator of Icelandic legends or advocate of German music. From his travels, he bought back with him to his London lodgings a great many objects to manifest and memorialise his new cosmopolitan identity. He surrounded himself with bohemian friends such as the 'fleshly' poet Algernon Charles Swinburne and the ostracised painter Simeon Solomon, and eventually became the stuff of hearsay and legend. A young Guy de Maupassant, one of the visitors at Powell's aforementioned cottage on the Normandy coast, wrote about the bizarre goings-on in that place, speculations that continue to fascinate writers and artists to this day. As a result, Powell has been called 'eccentric', 'sinister' and 'sad', words that tell us more about the judges – and the historical moment of judgement – than about the man being judged. Few have troubled themselves to consider Powell's contributions to Welsh culture.

Not that attempts to recognise such contributions are necessarily productive or advantageous. The literary scholar Raymond Garlick once tried to acknowledge Powell's juvenile verse, which was circulated mainly among friends and family, by naming its writer alongside Anglo-Welsh poets George Herbert, John Dyer and Dylan Thomas. To this, critic

David Lewis Jones responded that an 'Anglo-Welsh tradition' of poetry that 'must include figures like Powell seems to be worthless'. According to Jones, it is 'impossible to detect any meaningful Anglo-Welsh traits' in Powell, 'other than that he was Welsh (albeit a member of the anglicized gentry) and wrote in English'. Just which 'Anglo-Welsh traits' are 'meaningful', and who gets to decide? To some chroniclers of Wales, Powell's refusal or inability to fit a presumably Welsh profile constitutes a betrayal of his heritage. He 'spent a fortune promoting the customs and heritage of Iceland,' argued Russel Davies, 'but for the culture and history of the land that gave him his wealth, his heart was just as ice.'

In fact, as I will point out in my essay for *Queer Wales*, Powell expended considerable effort to ensure that the collection of books and artefacts he amassed during his short lifetime would come to Aberystwyth. He supported a number of local causes, served as president of the Aberystwyth Literary Institute and Working Men's Reading Room, and contributed money toward the rebuilding of the ancient St Padarn's church at Llanbadarn Fawr near Aberystwyth, where members of the Powell family are buried. As a pianist, Powell participated in several concerts at Aberystwyth's Assembly Rooms and presided over the 'Penny Readings and Musical Entertainment' in the town's Temperance Hall. To be sure, those were not occasions to celebrate Welsh culture for Powell, who performed the works of German Romanticism such as Schumann's 'Einsame Blume'. Powell was an authority on and an advocate of contemporary German music. The nineteenth-century English composer John Stainer, for instance, credited Powell with having 'converted' him to Schumann. As his collection confirms, whatever influence Powell had or sought to exert on Welsh culture came from without rather than within Wales.

Clearly, Powell wanted to be remembered as a man of the world, as a patron and benefactor. To affirm the validity of his act of self-fashioning, it was important to him to have the name he made – or remade – for himself stated and perpetuated. He may have intended to father children, being that, in 1881, he married a housekeeper from a village near

Fishguard; but the union produced no offspring and Powell died the following year. His collection became his legacy, and as such it was offered first to the council and then to the university.

Ingratiating himself to Principal Edwards by calling the university 'quite the worthiest and most intelligent corporate body' of Aberystwyth, Powell hoped that academics might be better able to appreciate its value. Indeed, the bequest was welcomed. Taking stock of it shortly after Powell's death, Professor J Mortimer Angus of University College Wales, Aberystwyth marvelled that it would be long before we 'exhaust' its 'treasures… and longer still before we forget Mr Powell's generosity to our College Library and Museum.' And yet, he declared, it was 'not easy to form a just idea of the collection', temporarily housed as it was in the college storerooms. Once again, no space was made available that was 'adequate to the proper display of the Powell Collection'. Angus thought it was 'a further incentive' to complete work on the building. The future Exam Hall, which then was a 'howling wilderness, where the fowls of the air have their nests, would make an admirable "Powell Museum"' – 'at once a tribute to Mr Powell's memory, and a fresh attraction to the town.' The 'Powell Museum' was never built. Was Powell perhaps too different, I wonder, too wayward – in more than one sense – to have been granted a space in which to contemplate his queerness?

Today, certain individual works in the bequest are much sought after and highly valued; but, the exhibition *Queer Tastes* aside, they are rarely shown in recognition of their collector. Neil Holland, curator of the School of Art collection at Aberystwyth University, pointed out that, considered as part of a whole, the objects forming the Powell bequest are 'imbued' with the collector's particular worldview; taken individually, on the other hand, they are rendered mute. Perhaps, it takes a kindred spirit to make even minor works in the collection speak for Powell. To me, such an item is the decidedly unacademic *Book of Wonderful Characters*, an anthology that promised readers the stories of men who 'essentially differed from the rest of the human race', whether due to 'some peculiar congenital defect' or owing to an 'eccentricity of character' that 'inevitably impels them to... trespass from the boundaries of... conventional life.' In it, Powell would have encountered the transvestite Chevalier d'Eon, based on whose case Havelock Ellis coined the term 'eonism'. After all, the word 'homosexual' – and the discrimination and pathologising to which it gave rise – was not used during Powell's lifetime.

Resisting our system of classification, Powell remains a marginal figure, which is to say that he has been relegated to the margins by historians or custodians of culture who don't know how to place him or refuse to make room for him. As I put it in *(Im)memorabilia,* a curatorial showcase of my own ephemera-stuffed closet that I once found the nerve to make at Aberystwyth University's School of Art galleries, private collections like Powell's may 'communicate intimate truths or express longings that cannot be articulated otherwise.' Their public display in an institution of culture and learning bespeaks a desire to come clean, to reach out and belong. Quite literally, showing off all we possess – be it of 'bigotry' or 'virtue' – means to declare 'I matter'. Ultimately, then, opening up to a squirearchical 'misfit' like Powell enables us to conceive of the ways in which lives lived in a far from homogeneous culture like that of Wales may matter differently.

Harry Heuser (PhD, City University of New York, 2004) is a writer, educator and curator. He is the author of *Immaterial Culture: Literature, Drama and the American Radio Play, 1929–1954.* Together with his husband, Robert Meyrick, he has written on English and Welsh art, including monographs of painters Claudia Williams and Gwilym Prichard, and is curating art exhibitions at Aberystwyth University, as well as the Royal Academy of Arts in London. His essay, 'Please Don't Whip Me *This* Time: The Passions of George Powell of Nant-Eos [sic]', will appear in the anthology *Queer Wales*, forthcoming from the University of Wales Press next year.

writer's
diary
2016
'With the diary beside me on my desk, I always feel like I have good company to hand'
Peggy Riley
'An inspiring companion for the emerging writer'
Fiona Sampson

2016
mslexia

SOMERSAULT

COMING OF AGE MEMOIR BY **DAI GEORGE**

THIS YEAR IT TURNED TEN YEARS SINCE MY LAST IN SCHOOL. IT WAS THE year of new driving licenses, Stax soul, and Liverpool's epic Champions League comeback against AC Milan: in many ways the happiest of my life so far, though in other more important respects my saddest. When I cast back to that foolish, pivotal year – poised flaccidly, in the wider view, between Britain's invasion of Iraq and the global economic meltdown five years later – I see a carful of boys in £80 jeans being disgorged outside the Rec. We've been ferried over by one of our tolerant fathers, who bids us goodnight and winds down his window, ventilating the Peugeot after the toxic shock of our collective aftershave. On the other side of the Rec door lies the eighteenth party we've been building up to in the common room all week, through endless, circular bouts of pre-match analysis over Shithead, a card game.

'Going to Bobby Davis'?'

'Yeah mate, course. Should be a big one.'

'Wanna warm up at mine?'

'Nah – might have some munch at home first and get a lift with my dad. Could pick you up, if you want?'

'Yeah, go on then. Shithead.'

'Ah, fuck.'

For the two years of sixth form I lived among boys, all the time pining for escape to the holiday lands of girls. We were boys of little bawdiness or braggadocio, and certainly no overt sexism. We just prized our own company, to my despair, cleaving to an exclusive patter based around games and mealtimes: pool, Playstation, plates piled high on one side with frozen pizza, on the other with Dolmio-drenched pasta. We watched *Twin Town* on eternal loop and could quote it to each other verbatim.

'Hot dogs for tea, boys bach!'
'Alright? Is Bryn in?'

Some of our number had girlfriends, so could afford a laissez-faire attitude to being near girls. They would stay with the group for as long as they were able before wandering off with their Saras and Lydias, leaving me stranded among the singletons. To make a beeline for someone I fancied, at school or at a party, seemed a manoeuvre on a par with strafing through no man's land. I felt sure that someone would notice and gun me down.

Ellie was worth the risk. On blessed lunchtimes I'd come down from lessons to see her sitting somewhere nearer to me than the Shithead society, and I'd pounce on the opportunity, pulling up a chair before anyone else could call across the common room and deal me in. Ellie was clever, gentle and unfathomably pretty: ginger, lightly freckled, with long straight hair and cheekbones you could slice fruit with. She had a quiet way of paying attention to you that I could never quite return. As she offered her questions, recalling trivial information from previous conversations, I would blab, overstate and self-deprecate. In return, I received very little – mere scraps, really, such as the fact that she loved Björk and lived in Llanishen, near the leisure centre.

Her birthday was in May, when everyone was busy revising for A levels. I don't remember any build-up to it in the common room, and not all that many people went. I turned up to the Rec on my own, bearing gifts of a Rainer Maria Rilke parallel translation (like me, she was bound for Bristol; unlike me, to study German and History) and a CD compilation of REM's early years. Surrounded by a select group of close family and friends, she was happier than I'd ever seen her. The music and buffet were better than usual, and I succeeded in peeling her away for five minutes to wish her happy birthday and blab. She introduced me to a girl called Laura who went to a different school and afterwards spent most of the night at Ellie's side.

The end of A levels meant the end of school and the greatest party of them all, our prom, which promised a final, defining switch from the Rec to a Hilton function suite. Had we still possessed a common room, pre-match analysis would have been rife, but it found a way out nonetheless, in post-exam gatherings, on MSN Messenger, over screenings of *Twin Town*.

'Reckon Ms Davies will show up?'

'Course – she's a top girl.'

'What about Mr Baston?'

'Nah, he's Christian.'

'You taking a date?'

'Fuck, are you meant to? Thought that was just in films and that.'

'Sara's going with her mates so I'll ride with you – don't worry, lads.'

Before the prom came there was other exciting business to finalise. A pre-uni lads' holiday was in the offing, though because we were harmless, ambivalent lads at best, we weren't going to Magaluf or anywhere like that. We were going to Copenhagen, where a family friend of Ga's had a flat. None of us knew much about Copenhagen, but so what? A lads' holiday – it was gonna be big.

On the day of the prom, we turned up at Eddy Hampson's in Rhiwbina to put on our suits and skull a few warm-up beers. The limo pulled up at half-five and took us on a long circuit of mams and dads, who all took photos of us in our finery and palmed beers into our hands, so that by the time we got to the Hilton we had a hefty surplus that had to be left with the driver as a tip.

Ms Davies came. As predicted, Mr Baston didn't. Towards the end of the night I took a blurry, unlit photo – a selfie, *avant la lettre* – of Ms Davies and me on the dancefloor, both of us squeezing into the frame of my new camera phone like sweethearts at the seaside. Other than that, the Hilton part of the evening passed without anything happening, in a blur of midrange wedding food, valedictory melodrama and '(I've Had) The Time of My Life'. We were all waiting for the after party at Eddy's. As soon as the lights went up, we said hasty goodbyes to the teachers and spilled out into fifty cabs.

I don't say this lightly: it was the best party ever. Others who went may disagree, but for me it's not even a question. The place was full, that's all I know, with every tribe of the common room intermingling, copping off, bursting out into the garden. I didn't cop off; I had something better. While the party raged around me, I sat on the floor of Eddy's sitting room with Ellie. All we did was talk, about Bristol and REM, Björk and existentialism, the future we could good as touch.

I took a second photo on my phone that night. This time I wasn't in it but Ellie was, along with my mate Les. In the corner of the picture, the grey-blue morning can be seen gathering above Eddy Hampson's gable. Though the party has finally wound up, we're all heading to Les', where we're going to nurse a last whisky and coke and watch *Twin Town*. Later we would fall asleep in front of the TV, cuddled up in our suits and frocks.

The next morning Ellie left before I woke. When I came to, I called a taxi to drive me home. I'm not sure if I'd ever done an all-nighter before, and I felt like warm putty, disoriented from booze and lack of sleep but soft, aglow. That feeling lasted all of twenty minutes, the time it took to be driven from Whitchurch to Canton and stagger smiling through the front door.

My parents and two sisters were gathered round the kitchen table with haggard, tearful faces.

'Gran's had a stroke,' Dad said. 'We didn't want to call and spoil your night.'

Her death caught me off guard. I couldn't cry. For my father and middle sister it was a catastrophe: she was the woman who'd nurtured Dad through an exemplary working-class boyhood, baking him Welsh cakes and folding his laundry, from pit town grammar school to Oxford. He adored her and everything she stood for, and her loss struck him with the whirlwind force of an orphaning. Catrin, my sister, had no less close a relationship. From the age of seven, she'd taken the train up to Treorchy during half terms to spend the week there with Gran, just shopping, drinking tea and playing dominoes. For me, even a weekly Sunday visit was pushing it: however much I loved her, I couldn't hack the bumpy Rhondda roads, and thoughts of the rare adventures my mates would be enjoying back in Cardiff played in my mind all afternoon. For the last year of her life, accelerated by the advent of hangovers, those Sunday visits dwindled until Gran took on the distant shape of an admonition: a paradigm of Valleys sacrifice and generosity, presiding over my everyday world of Cardiffian foolishness.

While Dad and Catrin retreated into heavy mourning, I tried to rally spirits. I cooked roasts for the family and broadcast consolatory tunes. Submerged in my weird, weak grief was the less edifying thought that all this death was inconvenient. It was the summer between A levels and uni and I had plans. Copenhagen had been paid for and came after the funeral, so there was no quarrel there – I'd go, with however heavy a heart. In the meantime, though, there were house parties, beach trips and gigs, every one of them a rich harvest of girls and liberty. Some of these I had no choice but to renounce, and in my listless mood sometimes I didn't even want to go. But others I was determined not to give up, and one of those was the REM concert in the Millennium Stadium on the eve of Gran's funeral.

Dad and Catrin were meant to come but had lost their appetite for gigs. They gave up their tickets free of charge, and I promptly called Ellie. She knew about my bereavement and I gulped down her condolences like they were sherbet dips. She said of course she'd come – but could she bring her friend Laura, too, who was a big REM fan? With two spare tickets, I was happy to offer my largesse.

On the night of the gig, Ellie and Laura showed up holding hands. I don't remember much else about it, except that the crowd only filled half the stadium so they brought the stage forward, and during the first song – 'What's the Frequency, Kenneth?' – Laura tilted Ellie's face back and kissed her.

The next morning I put on my prom suit, now accessorised with a plain black tie, and took my last nauseating car journey to 47 Dumfries Street. Sitting on the pouffe in her front room, I looked out through the back window on the view Gran had known all her life: a view that led past her washing line, her patch of garden, the defunct outhouse which used to house the loo, and up towards the tan heather of the mountain. Around me the wider family condoled and took out cling-filmed plates of sandwiches and quiche for the buffet after the service.

The difference between a hearse and a limo is tiny when you think about it. In the space a coffin takes up, you could easily fit eight lads in their new suits and still have room to pass round a complimentary bottle of Cava. To follow Gran's hearse, the family piled into yet more stretched black cars and trundled up Cemetery Road until we reached Gran's corrugated chapel, where mourners were already spilling onto the pavement for lack of room inside. We walked through the sombre ranks to the front row, and as soon as I sat I broke down into shuddering, raw, animal tears.

Copenhagen was damp and cool, not a million miles from Cardiff if you ignored the pastel architecture, the price of a pint and the harbour front where you could bring a pack of Tuborg and dangle your legs over the walls at night. The flat we'd inherited was airy and opulent beyond our wildest imaginings. We liked the rest of the city but couldn't afford it, so channelled our resources into a blowout Saturday night on the town. In the warm-up drinks beforehand, someone was hogging the bathroom, with Worky desperate for a piss. Worky banged on the door but the hogger wouldn't relent, so he dashed out to the sixth-floor kitchen window and released his burden lavishly onto the courtyard below. I took a photo of it on my phone: he's kneeling prayerfully on the kitchen counter with his back to the room, head tilted heavenwards in relief.

Once out on the Copenhagen streets, we put into action a plan to pretend that we were all in a band on tour – the idea being that if we got any girls to come back to our rock star flat with us, the flat would be proof enough to clinch the lie. Miraculously the plan worked, and two beautiful Danish girls – women? – followed us home for the after party.

Sometime between then and daybreak the mood soured. After blacking out from vodka, I remember surfacing in the living room, with Duffy kissing one of the women on the sofa while I berated Eddy Hampson, howling at him about the depth of my loss, my love for Gran, and the shallowness of modern life. Reaching for the dinky Spanish guitar that was our only other rock star prop, I strummed a tune and tried to sing, but the words proved impossible. Eddy said he was going to bed, leaving me alone with the couple on the sofa and the other woman. I blacked out again.

When I woke, both women were gone. Everyone else was still asleep, though it must have been lunchtime at the earliest. I grabbed my wallet and phone and slipped out of the flat into a flood of reproving sunshine.

My first port of call was a corner shop, where I handed over a 100 Kroner note for a six-pack of Tuborg. Next, I went to a park. I drank all afternoon, topping up my levels from the night before, and I wept. Around me, the beautiful people of Copenhagen were pushing buggies and playing frisbee, enjoying their Sunday. I wish I could say it was the first time I ever understood the terrific, terrifying effect of alcohol on a broken heart – how it consoles and exacerbates your every pang, causing the hours to blur and fall away – but that would be a lie. It was, however, the first time I understood how those effects could be bought and sold at any time of day, if you were only prepared to slacken your willpower and abandon hope. I wept doubly, for the futility of loving Ellie and the lost view from Gran's window. I wept for the solidarity, betterment and pride that Treorchy was meant to represent for me, and did, though I hardly knew how. I wept for the squandered last conversation with Gran at her hospital bedside, when she lay comatose beside me and all I'd spoken of was Ellie and my summer plans. I wept until a text came through from Ga.

Where r u? Worried mate.

I texted back with the name of the park. The boys found me, a drunken wreck, and propped me on my feet.

'Don't worry, son – one that got away, eh?'

'Yeah, can't all get lucky as Duff.'

'Fit, though, weren't they?'

'Aye, not bad.'

'Game of keep-ups?'

We knocked about the football, with my contribution more shambolic than usual, before heading back to the flat to watch *Con Air*.

The following morning, our last in Copenhagen, I was treated with delicate care. We had a sober day of activities lined up, starting with a trip to the city's Royal Library, followed by the Islandsbrygge Havnebad, or Harbour Bath. I have a recurring nightmare of deep water: a dream where I'm flung into a vast lake, never to surface. Though they meant for our North Sea swim to be fun and restorative, my friends had unknowingly recreated that very nightmare.

While they plunged one by one into the water, I malingered onshore with a book. I started to feel their scorn, almost as a physical presence. I was sure they thought I'd tipped over into milking it – that my small appetite for banter and games had become a lame expression of martyrdom. Chastened, I put the book down and made my way over to the towering diving point.

Teetering on the edge, with a queue forming behind me, I toyed with the idea of jumping versus walking back through the crowd and sitting it out. The summer and life beyond it had taken a turn for the worse. I was stuck in a multidimensional no man's land, clueless as to how to put it right. Stuck between Ellie and the next impossible passion. Stuck between a solid Welsh childhood, which had run aground, and the unmoored possibilities of life across the Severn Bridge. Stuck between this savage virginal loneliness and the company of my beautiful friends swimming below.

In a moment of blankness I jumped and tumbled to the sea. The water smashed the wind out of me and foamed over my head, briny and freezing cold. The sheer oblivion of it amazed me. I willed myself to stay down there, in my nightmare, for as long as I could, until my body's buoyancy won out and hoisted me up for air.

Dai George's debut poetry collection, *The Claims Office*, was published by Seren.

FAMILY

STORY BY **JEM POSTER**

He'd slept badly, as he always did at his parents' house, and had woken to find Anna propped on one elbow, staring into his face.

'What is it?' he asked.

'You were whimpering.'

'Whimpering?'

'Like this.' She made a high, childlike noise in the back of her throat. 'You must have been dreaming.' She swept her tangled hair back from her face and leaned forward to kiss him.

Daniel took the kiss absently. 'Maybe I was,' he said. There was something there at the back of his mind, but not an image, nothing he could lay hold of; just a faint sense of unease.

'That's not a kiss.' She pressed her mouth hard against his and ran her hand slowly down his belly. He stiffened at her touch.

'I forgot to bring them,' he said. 'The condoms.'

'We could take the risk.'

He lay still, saying nothing.

'It wouldn't matter,' she said at last. 'Your mum's desperate for grandchildren. She told me so.'

'When did she say that?'

'Yesterday. When we were in the kitchen making the tea. She says she wants us to have children while she's still young enough to appreciate them.' She nestled closer, settled her chin in the dip behind his collarbone. 'It would give meaning to her life, she says – a new family, everything starting again.'

He'd been unable to explain to Anna just what it was about that revelation – his mother's longing breathed into his ear like an obscene secret – that had unmanned him. He put his arms around her, feeling with a pained detachment the shifting pressure of her body against his own, but after a few moments he turned away and buried his face in the pillow.

Bad start. And later, when breakfast was over and his mother was washing the dishes at the sink, his father set down his teacup, rose heavily from his chair and leaned over him. 'A quick word,' he said, 'if you have a moment.'

'What about?'

Mr Collett glanced at his wife's bent back. 'Not here,' he whispered, shaking his head. He led the way out of the breakfast room and into his study, conspiratorial and subtly coercive. 'A favour,' he said, reaching behind Daniel's back to push the door shut. 'A little errand.'

'What kind of errand?'

His father stepped over to his desk, opened the top drawer and drew out a clump of tissue paper. He placed it on the surface and began to tug at it with clumsy fingers. 'I bought this' – he extracted a small object and held it out towards Daniel – 'when we were on our honeymoon.'

He remembered it from his childhood, one of his mother's dressing-table curiosities: a faceted scent bottle, elaborately but tastelessly decorated. Around its body, a circle of plump cherubs in tarnished silver, pointing their toes and straining upward on their feathered wings; set slightly asquint in the cap and winking now in the wintry light as his father turned the bottle in his fingers, a single crudely cut topaz.

'What's that got to do with me?' There was a trace of aggression, not quite unintentional, in the question.

'I want to give it to her again. Replenished.' He lingered on the word, and Daniel realised, with a faint queasiness, that his father had conceived of this second giving as a reconsecration. He would offer the little vial to his wife as an emblem of love's restoration after years of dryness. 'I wondered...'

'If I'd buy the perfume?'

'If you wouldn't mind.' His father placed the bottle reverently on the desktop. He drew out his wallet and counted out three five-pound notes. '*Folle de Toi*. That's what she always used to wear.'

It had been years since his mother had worn perfume, but he remembered her sweeping into the room one evening while the babysitter was reading to him, the fragrance enveloping him as she stooped to kiss him goodnight. It was a memory he'd clung to: his mother radiant as he'd never seen her since, his father unaccountably absent.

'I shouldn't think they make it any more,' he said, snatching up the notes and stuffing them into his top pocket.

*

'You shouldn't let it get to you,' said Anna, watching him in the mirror as she brushed her hair. 'He's asked you to do something for him, that's all.'

'I'm not his fucking servant.'

'Daniel, please – there's no point. Just go. Twenty minutes into town, twenty minutes finding the stuff, back by eleven. Better than spending the whole day fuming.'

'The thing is,' said Daniel with careful emphasis, as though explaining a self-evident fact to one of his denser pupils, 'it's always like this. Christmas, birthdays, anniversaries – he finds someone else to do the job. Always. When did he last buy her anything – I mean, actually go into a shop and choose something for her?'

'He hates shops. They make him uncomfortable. You know how he is.'

'Shopping's a fact of life. And when it comes to presents, it shouldn't matter whether he likes it or not. There's a principle involved.'

Anna banged down the brush and turned to face him. 'Give me the money,' she said. She reached out her hand. 'If it's such a trial to you, I'll get the bloody perfume.'

Exasperated but sensible; an adult response. And he was a child again, hurt and cross, hugging his grievance close. He grabbed his coat from the chair he'd slung it on. 'No,' he said, brushing past her, refusing to meet her gaze. 'No, I'll do it.'

*

There was a time, he thought, swinging out of the drive and accelerating away from the house, when his arguments with Anna had meant something. He remembered storms of vituperative passion and, in their aftermath, hours or even days in which, it seemed to him, they loved with a renewed delicacy and tenderness. Now, just these inconclusive spats and the dull fretfulness that followed. As he reached the edge of the village, he slammed the car into fifth and put his foot down hard.

Parking in town had been difficult for as long as he could remember, and the years since his departure had seen a marked increase in tourist traffic. Now the narrow streets were jammed morning to evening, the car parks almost invariably full. But he found a space down behind the cinema, a gap barely longer than the car, between a builder's truck and an awkwardly angled motorcycle. He had thirty minutes: more than enough. He checked his watch and stepped out briskly towards the high street, feeling his mood lighten as he walked. Something, he thought, to do with the finding of the parking space; something to do with his being even now, after more than a decade in London, a local boy, possessed of local knowledge. He knew the backstreets; he knew the one shop that might still stock an outmoded perfume.

But Morrell's was gone. The ornate window-frame and doorway were unchanged, but the space beyond was unfamiliar, a long, pale gallery lined with watercolours.

'Two years ago,' said the woman behind the desk. 'A few months after the new place opened. Morrell's couldn't compete.'

'Where would I find the new place?'

'In the mini-mall. The Beauty Spot.' She scribbled the name on a pink Post-it and handed it to him. 'Left out of the door, fifty yards up on your right.'

He'd seen the mall on earlier visits but had never set foot in it. A monstrosity, his father had insisted when it first went up, though in fact the entrance was entirely unexceptionable – a red-brick façade not dissimilar in style to the buildings on either side and suitably proportioned. But the interior, he saw now, was another matter, a mock piazza in glossy pink marble with a dribbling fountain at its centre.

The Beauty Spot had pretensions, no doubt of it. You stepped beyond the open shelves of middle-range cosmetics at the shop's entrance into a space dominated by the wide curve of a glass display counter stocked with famously expensive brands. Behind the counter stood a woman slim as a mannequin, immaculately dressed in black with a triple-stranded choker of small pearls encircling her throat; his mother's age, Daniel guessed, but still radiating a muted, knowing sexuality. There was nobody else in the shop and the sudden hush as the door fell shut was faintly unnerving.

'I'm looking for a perfume,' he said. 'An older brand. *Folle de Toi*.'

The woman mouthed the words. 'Yes,' she said. 'I remember it. Rich. Musky. Very seventies.'

'Exactly. Do you stock it?'

She gave him a thin, glossy smile. 'I think you'll find it was discontinued long ago. I can check if you like.' She turned away and began to tap at a keyboard, her head bowed so that her straight, discreetly highlighted hair fell forward, curtaining her face. And something in the line of her bent neck, in the swell of the vertebrae between the choker's silver clasp and the collar of her dress, stirred him to an agony of inappropriate desire.

'No,' she said after a moment, turning back to face him. 'It's not coming up. I can more or less guarantee that you won't find it.' She spread her manicured hands on the counter-top. 'Would you like me to suggest an alternative?'

His mouth was dry. 'It's for my mother,' he said.

'Well, you have two options: you could go for something similar, or you might like to consider something a little more – how old is your mother?'

'Fifty-three.'

'I'd suggest something brighter, more floral. The heavier perfumes –'

'I need as close a match as you've got. Sentimental reasons.'

'Of course.' She squatted down behind the counter and slid back a door. 'You have to bear in mind,' she said, 'that I'm working from memory as far as the original fragrance is concerned. But I think you'll find this comes fairly close.' She bobbed up again, with a small atomiser in her hand. 'Similar in general tone, but perhaps a shade more complex.' She rested her free hand palm upward on the counter and puffed a tiny cloud of perfume onto her wrist. 'We'll just wait a second or two.'

He sniffed the air. 'I'm getting it. Not quite what I remember, but...'

'You need to smell it on skin. It makes a difference.' She raised her arm and held it outstretched towards him.

He bent his head obediently and breathed in. She moved her wrist closer to his face, so close that he could feel the warmth of her on his own skin. 'Try now,' she said.

He inhaled again. And it might have been the effect of the perfume or the strange intimacy of the transaction, but in the instant before she withdrew her arm he had an unsettling sense of space and exposure, as if he were looking out over some wild, vertiginous landscape.

'What do you think?' she asked. 'There are a couple of others we might try.'

He glanced at his watch. 'No,' he said. 'This one will be fine.'

'I don't think you'll do better. If that's the kind of thing you want.' She turned and took a small crimson box from one of the shelves behind her. 'That'll be forty-five pounds.'

'Forty-five?'

She gave him a reproachful look. 'You won't find it for less,' she said.

He tugged his wallet from his pocket and extracted a credit card. 'Would you like me to gift-wrap it?' she asked. 'There'd be no extra charge.'

'Thank you, but there's no need.' His hand, he realised as he held out the card for her to take, was trembling uncontrollably, but if she noticed she gave no sign of it.

*

Mr Collett was at his desk, poring over a gardening catalogue, when Daniel entered. He slid his reading glasses a fraction lower on his long nose and peered over the lenses. 'Success?'

'Yes and no. The line's been discontinued, but I've managed to get hold of something similar.' Daniel slipped the box from his pocket and placed it on the desk beside his mother's scent bottle.

'You've tried everywhere?'

'I had someone check it out for me. It's definitely unobtainable.'

'Well,' said Mr Collett, and paused just long enough for Daniel to feel the weight of his disappointment. 'I suppose we shall have to make do. Any change?'

'It cost a little more than you'd reckoned.'

'Then I owe you.' Mr Collett dug into his trouser pocket and pulled out a handful of coins. 'How much?'

Daniel shook his head. 'It doesn't matter.'

'That's kind of you.' Mr Collett returned the coins to his pocket. 'And one more kindness, if you wouldn't mind.' He took the box and the empty scent bottle from the desk-top and held them out. 'A fiddly job,' he said, 'and my eyesight's not what it was.'

Daniel felt the anger rising in him again. Was there no end to it? – the imposition on those around him of simple, practical tasks that any grown man should have been ashamed to delegate. Why were they still letting him get away with it? For a second or two he entertained the possibility of refusal; then he reached out and took the objects from his father's hands.

He was halfway up the stairs when his mother came out into the hallway, wiping her palms on the bib of her apron. 'Lunch in half an hour,' she said, and then, lowering her voice: 'There's nothing wrong, is there, Daniel?'

'Wrong?' He stopped and leaned over the stair-rail.

'Between you and Anna. She went rushing out just after you left, without a word to me. That's not like her.'

'She probably wanted a bit of time to herself.' His mother stood staring up at him, her face dark with unspoken questions. 'Really,' he said, moving on up the stairs. 'There's nothing wrong.'

The upstairs heating was off and the bedroom was cold. He switched on the light, sat down at the dressing-table and pushed Anna's brush, comb and eyeliner to one side. Then he placed the crimson box in the centre of the cleared space and unscrewed the cap of his mother's scent bottle.

Beneath the cap, a little rubber stopper. He eased it out and placed it carefully on the polished surface and, as he did so, he caught, rising from the aperture, the ghost of that older fragrance, sweeter than its replacement and less overtly sexual. He raised the bottle to his nose and took a deep breath, drawing her to him across three decades: a girl in her twenties, her hair still dark and falling in loose curls to the shoulders of her embroidered blouse, her face unlined. He saw her leaning towards him – at the kitchen table, it might have been, or out on the lawn beneath the towering hollyhocks – and felt, with a sharp jolt of surprise, the tears prickling behind his eyelids.

He set the bottle aside and took up the box. The new perfume – he knew it without having to smell it again – was a travesty. He could return it to the shop, it occurred to him, return it and get his money back. For perhaps half a minute he sat there, weighing up the implications; then, with a quick, emphatic movement, he ripped back the flap.

The new bottle might have been designed as a reproach to the decorative excesses of the old: its clean contours fitted his hand snugly and the cap, a clear plastic globe as neat as a berry, turned easily between his finger and thumb. He removed the stopper and drew his mother's bottle towards him again.

It should have been obvious from the outset, but it was only when he began to transfer the perfume that he realised what he'd let himself in for. There was no flow, just an impeded oozing of liquid from one aperture to the other. Little by little the perfume pooled in the bottom of the lower bottle, but he could see that almost as much was running down its outer surface, channelling itself behind the silverwork and dripping onto the dressing-table. The waste, he thought, the stupid bloody waste of time and money; but he kept at it, rigid with concentration and suppressed fury.

He hadn't heard Anna return and she startled him, entering the room in stockinged feet and leaning suddenly over his shoulder. 'Do you want me to shut the door?' she asked. She fanned her hand across her face. 'This stuff's strong. You can smell it from the hallway.'

'Close it as you go out.'

'I wanted to say sorry.'

'Sorry?' He adjusted the angle of the inverted bottle. 'Sorry for what?'

'For this morning. Your dad's difficult, I know that, and I didn't help matters.'

'It's not worth discussing.'

She placed her hand gently on his shoulder. 'You're still wearing your coat,' she said. She bent and unbuttoned the collar, brushing the side of his face with her lips. 'Your mum says to tell you lunch will be ready in five minutes.'

'I have to finish this. I'll be down when I'm done.'

She peered more closely at the bottles. 'It looks almost impossible,' she said. 'Couldn't you do with more light?' She stepped over to the bedside table and picked up the lamp.

'Leave it,' he said, looking up over his shoulder. 'The flex is too short.'

She hesitated, but brought the lamp over. 'Just long enough,' she said, perching it on the edge of the dressing-table. One of Mrs Collett's car-boot purchases: an ugly piece vaguely modelled on an oil lamp, with a sprigged porcelain base and a bulbous shade of streaky pink glass.

'It's not safe there.'

'You can move it as soon as you've finished.' She clicked the switch. 'Isn't that better?' She was hanging over him again. 'What you really need for that job,' she said, 'is a hypodermic syringe.'

He banged the bottle down on the dressing-table. 'For fuck's sake, Anna. Where am I going to get a hypodermic syringe?'

'I'm just trying to be helpful.' And it was true, he thought, she only wanted to make things right. He heard his mother open the breakfast room door and bustle to the foot of the stairs.

'I'm serving up,' she shouted.

Daniel frowned. 'Go on,' he said. 'Tell her I'll be down soon.'

'Come down now. You can finish that later.'

He shook his head and turned back to his task, catching again as he leaned forward, but so fleetingly that he couldn't be sure he hadn't imagined it, the faint sweetness he'd picked up earlier.

Anna was moving away. 'Don't be long, then,' she said. 'You know what she's like.'

The door clicked shut. He bent low over the dressing-table and drew a deep breath. Nothing now but the dark, cloying notes of the new perfume. He sniffed the air again in a kind of panic, desperate for a trace of the lost fragrance; then he swung his right arm viciously outward, sweeping the lamp to the floor.

Later, he would return to the moment, interrogating an action that seemed neither merely accidental nor entirely voluntary; but now he simply sat and stared at the scatter of broken glass while the rage drained out of him.

'What was that?' He heard Anna hurrying back across the landing.

She threw open the door and started towards him, but came to a dead halt at the edge of the debris. 'What happened?'

'I caught it with my sleeve.'

She balanced on one foot and brought the other up to rest against her thigh; a rosette of blood was blooming through the sole of her sock.

'Let me see that,' he said.

She touched the bloodstain with her fingertips. 'It's nothing.' Her voice was small and dull. She wavered, set her foot awkwardly to the floor.

'Take your sock off. There might be glass in the cut.'

'It's nothing,' she repeated.

He wanted to go to her but his mother was calling again, shrill and insistent.

'Yes,' he shouted back. He rose stiffly to his feet and began to unbutton his coat. 'Yes, we're on our way.'

But Anna was down on her knees, trying to align the edges of two of the larger fragments. Her hands were shaking; he heard, beneath the rhythm of her breathing, the brittle whisper of glass on glass. After a moment she sat back on her heels and looked up at him, acknowledging with an almost imperceptible shrug of her shoulders that the thing was beyond mending.

Jem Poster is the author of a poetry collection, *Brought to Light* (Bloodaxe, 2001), and two novels, *Courting Shadows* and *Rifling Paradise* (Sceptre, 2002 and 2006). A third novel is in progress, and he has recently completed editing volume 3 of the six-volume Oxford University Press *Edward Thomas: Prose Writings*.

MR WOLF

STORY BY **ANNA LEWIS**

I WAS ONLY ONE PERSON, AND EVEN THAT WAS OFTEN TOO MANY. Sometimes I just had to walk downstairs and my father would break out of his study, demanding to know who had let a herd of elephants loose, or I had only to sit at the table and eat my breakfast to be told that it was no wonder half the world was starving.

My father was two people, and he was adored for it. John Walton was the name his parents had given him, and the name he gave to me, sort of: I'm Timothy John Walton. My mother called him John, although I don't think I ever heard him call her anything in return, and nor did he ever use my name with me. Henry Wolf was the name he chose for himself, the name on all the covers of his books.

The whole time that Glenda worked for us, she called him Mr Wolf. My mother never corrected her. I never saw Glenda address my father directly, but she would ask my mother: which shirts does Mr Wolf want ironed? Should I clean Mr Wolf's study? What time do you expect Mr Wolf to be home? Dusting the bookshelves, she moved more slowly over the shelf with my father's books, dusting each one individually and very lightly, folding the cloth first to make sure that the part she used was clean. The first time, I stood on the sofa cushion to watch her, and when she reached that particular shelf I shouted, 'Those are my dad's books!'

She jumped. I explained: 'There are really only seven of them, but there are two copies of some and three of others, so altogether there are,' I couldn't remember, and had to count them again, 'seventeen.' She stared warily at the row of books as if they might throw themselves at her. The shelf was too high, so that whenever I wanted to look at his books I had to pull over a chair from the window. I was always careful to lift each volume out with two hands in case I dropped it. The same black-and-white photograph was on the back of each cover but the man in the photograph was clean-shaven and young. His gaze through the lenses of his glasses was straight and sure, with no suggestion of a smile.

'He was handsome, your dad, when he was young,' Glenda said.

'He doesn't look like that now.'

'No, I know.' We both glanced across the room to where my mother sat with a lapful of beads in the bay window: her malachite necklace. The stones clicked dully against each other as she slid them onto the new thread.

'Do you like books, like your dad?' Glenda asked.

'Very much, yes I do.'

'My daughter does too. She's about the same age as you. You know,' Glenda paused in her dusting and turned down towards me, 'when I told her I was going to work in the house of a real writer, a famous author, she didn't believe me at first. Now she's always asking if I can bring her here.'

I thought about it. 'I don't think my mum would mind.'

'I'm not sure.'

But she didn't mind: in fact, it would be nice for me to have a friend, and so Lexie arrived beside me on the sofa, a china plate in one hand and a ginger biscuit in the other, crumbs tumbling over the cushions and onto the floor.

'Lexie!' said Glenda. 'Who do you think is going to have to clean those crumbs up?' Lexie turned her head to look at me.

'Not Timothy, Lexie: me. You promised you would behave.' We

never, normally, ate biscuits in the sitting room. My mother looked uncertain whether to offer Lexie another, and without being asked, Glenda collected all of our plates and carried them into the kitchen.

I showed Lexie my bedroom, the television room, the back garden and the stream, the hollow in the bank where it was possible to sit without being seen from the house, but she only wanted to see my father's books. After Glenda had handed them down to her, she wanted to see inside his study.

No – never, no way. We can't. *Because.*

I was almost in tears by the time she reached out a hand to the doorknob. The door whispered open over the carpet, and a shrewd, dark smell – of coffee, cigarette smoke, sweat – edged out onto the landing. Sunlight fell through the net at the window as though through a mangle.

Behind his desk, Lexie ran her hands over the deep faces of the drawers, rolling her palms around their wooden knobs. She crouched at the wastepaper basket and plucked out a ball of paper, smoothed it over her knee, read a few words out loud and crumpled it again. She climbed up onto the chair, standing on the yellowed leather cushion and rattled the pens in the pen-pot. She drummed her palms on the polished wood then leant forward and reached for the typewriter. A sheet of paper stood upright in its wide mouth. In the doorway I said, 'Lexie – don't touch that, please.'

She rested her fingers lightly on the keys. 'What would I write, if I was a writer?'

'Lexie, don't.' Lexie hummed, lifted her fingers, and replaced them. 'Lexie, *please*.'

She looked up from the typewriter, down at me on the carpet. I could feel my jaw wobbling.

'I wasn't going to write anything,' she said. She climbed down, pushed the chair back into place under the desk, trotted across the floor and took up a corner of the net curtain. 'Oh, you can see the garden – the stream and the trees.' I nodded, rubbing my eyes. 'Over the fence into next door's garden, too.' She let the curtain fall. 'Come on,' she said. On the landing, she pulled the door closed behind us with both hands.

Lexie wore shorts that pretended to be a skirt: she proved it by trying to lift the skirt up and failing. Culottes. She wore shorts because, according to her mother, she was a tomboy. I, according to my father, was a nancy boy, which was not the same thing at all. My father was not pleased that my new friend was a little girl, until he met her. 'What a *charm*,' he said to my mother after Glenda and Lexie had gone.

After that, Glenda had to check with my mother whenever she wanted to bring Lexie to the house, to make sure that my father was in. He joined us for tea and cake in the sitting room, and took Lexie up to see his study. I peered around the doorjamb from the landing. She touched nothing, and nodded with polite fascination. 'Is that a typewriter, Mr Wolf?'

Her favourite joke was to creep up the stairs and knock at his study door, then call out, 'What's the time, Mr Wolf?' My father's favourite joke was to open his door, roll up his sleeve and look at his watch, then lean down towards Lexie and say, 'The time... is a quarter past... *three*!' before leaping forward, roaring and swinging his arms in the air. Lexie screamed and ran down the stairs, my father howling and clawing behind her. The first time this happened I was at the bottom of the staircase, half in and half out of the sitting room door and watching Lexie's ascent. At the moment of my father's roar, from the corner of my eye I saw my mother jump in the bay window, the beads spill from her lap. It was her amber necklace, that time, and I crawled around on the floor to help her retrieve the beads. We never quite found all of them. 'Where is Glenda?' my mother asked, sitting up on her heels, but neither of us had seen her since lunchtime.

'You have to look smart,' my mother said, combing out my parting and redrawing it for the third time, as though I would have preferred to look a mess. I wanted to look smarter than I had ever looked, older, richer, thinner, taller. She tapped lightly at my hands. 'Don't fiddle. When we're there, you will have to be good as gold – really on your best behaviour, darling. No fiddling, no fussing, no being silly.'

I had not been able to sleep for the last two nights, and had barely been able to eat breakfast that morning. My parents' bedroom door banged. Footsteps on the stairs: my father would in a moment be waiting for us in the hall. 'I'm ready Mummy, come on,' I said as she buttoned up my blazer, then unbuttoned it again.

'Alright. Come on now.' She held out her hand and led me downstairs. Her amber necklace, shorter than it had once been, glowed against her white dress. She smelled of vanilla, her hands soft. My father stood with his back to the front door and stared at both of us as we approached. 'The car is here,' he said.

I sat between my parents on the cream-coloured bench in the back, almost as long as our sofa. In the front seat a dark-skinned man in a grey uniform steered us smoothly through the evening, never once turning over his shoulder or saying a word. Around us lights went out in shop windows and came on in restaurants and pubs, green and red and gold; we glided past them in the growing dark. Crowds passed on the pavements, but no sound reached inside. My father watched, as I did, from the window, and my mother looked straight ahead.

We reached the brightly lit front of a shop, a large bookshop, its doors open and a woman in a tight black dress standing between them. My mother patted my hand. The dark-skinned man stopped the car and swung out, opened my father's door, and held it wide as my father stepped onto the pavement. I wriggled out after him. The man winked at me and I turned to look back at my mother, shifting sideways along the bench. My father was already standing beside the woman in the black dress, her head tilted to one side, thick blonde hair collapsing over her shoulder.

Inside the shop it felt like Christmas Eve. People, grown-ups, stood in smiling groups, each person holding a glass. Over their heads, cigarette smoke swayed gently. In the centre of the room, a table was piled with copies of a silver-jacketed hardback; I lifted one down, and saw my father's photograph on the back. This one, although still black and white, was different from that on all of the books in our house: it looked more like my father, with broad nose and beard. I took down one book, then another and another, turning each one over to the back: the same photograph on each.

A hand landed on my shoulder and stayed there. I looked up. A tall, thin woman asked: wouldn't I prefer to look at the books in the children's corner? No, I wouldn't. She began to re-pile the books I had taken down as I turned to look more carefully around the room. I was the only child. A fizzing sensation intensified in my chest.

'Will Lexie be there?' I had asked my mother when we were getting ready. My mother had laughed. 'Why would Lexie be there? No, darling.' And it was true, it seemed to be true. No Lexie, no one but me. I left the thin woman to her tower of books and skipped across the room to my mother, took her hand and drew myself tall beside her. She looked down at me and smiled, and the fizzing feeling grew thicker, higher inside me, fine bubbles spreading up into my shoulders and neck and down my arms. I swung my hand in hers, and as she kept talking to the people in her group, she let our hands swing and swing.

Later, my father stood by the table and read from one of the books, while everyone else in the room stood around him in silence, not even sipping from their glasses. I had never heard my father read a story before, and his voice was unfamiliar: at once deeper and quieter than usual, and huskier. As it rose and fell, it gave me the same feeling I had had in the back of the car as it curved around the corners, causing the three of us to tilt, slide upright, tilt again to the other side. I kept my hand in my mother's, and she kept her fingers rubbing gently across my skin. I don't recall anything of the story, but remember how when he had finished speaking, all of the people made, for a moment, small moaning and humming sounds before they began to clap. Then everyone began to move around the room again, more talking and smiling, more drinking, the gauze of smoke thickening, my father's face growing redder. I remember my mother carrying me through our front door, hearing her huff and puff a little, close to my ear, as she carried me up the stairs to my bedroom.

I didn't wake until morning, when I found myself in pure sunlight. My mother had not drawn my curtains: they hung aloof at each side of the window. I rolled out of bed and went to look down at the garden. Everything was very quiet. The water in the stream was low, and the leaves not waving even slightly on their branches.

I did not see Lexie again. Glenda never came back to our house, and I never asked my mother where they were or why they had stopped coming. Part of me was afraid that, if I asked, my mother would say: 'Oh – let me telephone Glenda.' I could hear her voice, see her hand on the receiver, her other hand pressing open the address book. Instead, I helped her to dust the mantelpiece, the cabinet, the bookshelves. She didn't take out each of my father's books and dust them separately, like Glenda did, but ran the cloth briskly over their spines. Sometimes we sang while we dusted, songs I had learnt at school, or songs that my mother made up.

Days passed, a week, and I did not see my father. One morning I crouched outside his study door and touched my ear to the wood, but was not sure whether I could hear anything. I thought there was a faint scuttling sound, a deep, distant drumming. Later, when I came home from school, I sat on the stairs just underneath the landing, took from my pockets the chocolates I had bought in the tuck shop that morning, and ate them there one after another. They were soft and sticky and warm. After putting each chocolate into my mouth, I smoothed out the wrapper and pushed it beneath the study door. Each shiny, sparkly square, green, pink and gold, crackled softly as it disappeared.

From the kitchen I heard my mother call my name. I pulled myself up by the banister, wiped my mouth on my sleeve, and ran towards her down the stairs.

Anna Lewis is the author of two poetry collections, *Other Harbours* (Parthian, 2012) and *The Blue Cell* (Rack Press, 2015).

SICILIAN DRIFTWOOD

STORY BY **ROBERT MINHINNICK**

For me he'll always be the *old man*. I found this in one of those Moleskine notebooks, part of that hoard he left. That almighty mess. We knew he was writing everything down but this is with dates and locations, as if he thought someone might read it. Or care about that indecipherable life he led.

You've seen some of his archive but new things keep turning up in unexpected places. Loose pages ripped from exercise books, scrawls on the backs of other people's letters. Some of you boys wiped your shitty arses with those pages and I'm still angry about that. But you know the stuff, how he arrived in Albania or got on a bus from Baghdad. Yes, why couldn't he have written a blog like everybody else?

Yet maybe his life is all too clear. Seems his condition was worse than we thought. Periods of delirium when the malaria came back, not to mention that incident he boasted about. This has a title too, 'The Satyr', and here's what I copied from the Moleskine. Honest, word for word.

*

'The Satyr'

They were in a favoured spot a few miles off the Tunisian coast. When they pulled up the net there was a leg in it. Along with the sardines and the anchovies there was a statue's leg.

On every expedition afterwards they thought maybe this time we'll get the whole body. And you know? They did. A year later this green creature was hauled over the side. The leg belonged to the body and the body to the leg. The crew of the Fat Captain *out of western Sicily had been proved right. But that's the Tunisian coast for you. Hidden wonders, and that statue as Greek as it gets.*

The five of us had felt like swifts, rising. That town was full of swifts but even when we reached the top and looked around we still didn't know where the voice was coming from. Until someone glanced up. And there she was, a young woman, beckoning.

Woo hoo! Here, here! *she was calling. So we climbed three flights and she said,* Please, come and look at this. I show all passing visitors.

This woman took us outside onto a balcony and we crowded in. The ones at the back couldn't understand but those in front realised straightaway what she wanted us to see.

It was the view. The frightening panorama from that apartment. The town is at a difficult altitude already but those buildings, tall themselves, had been constructed on the very summit. Only one of the churches stood above it. And so we looked straight out toward Etna.

Giddying, I tell you. Made me sick, it was so sudden. That was the top of the world and we were gazing across slopes of black lava at smoke from the volcano and that cloud that always seems to hang there. A double warning, I thought, that smoke, that cloud. But everyone seemed to take it as normal. Just like history, they ignored the dangers.

I think she was Romanian. Gave us all an almond biscuit, a thimble of coffee, and said in English, So what do you think?

Marvellous, *we said. Because she was clearly proud. This was her apartment and she was entertaining spur of the moment guests. Her spur, her moment. She said every morning she and her daughter ate breakfast on that balcony.*

I had to step away. Even when I braved a second look I needed to grasp the rail. The world I knew had vanished so there was nothing under my feet.

Maybe it's a sign of ageing but everything started to swim around me.

Later in the square people asked us where we were staying. We waited for one another to speak before it dawned that we didn't know the house's name.

With Beppe, *we said.* That's where. You must know Beppe. *But everyone we met in that square seemed to be called Beppe. It was St Anthony's Day and the women were preparing a feast. The men were already outside, the old men in the square at their tables, men who looked like they had been sitting there for a thousand years.*

Working in the square was a child. Ned, they called him, but I'm not sure if that was his name. He talked to us in English but said he spoke three languages, Italian, French, Arabic, and we believed him. So maybe that's four. When you're mono like I am it gets embarrassing. Too late now I thought, I'm plain stupid. Another form of vertigo.

This diary tells me exactly a year ago I became acquainted with the landscape of my own brain. Those photographs of a CT scan could have been a black walnut. My consultant pointed out two white patches, tracing them with a biro. He called them lesions.

How's the memory? *he asked.*

I had to think before I answered.

Fine, I replied. *And stared him down. Christ, even in that conversation I was trying to bluff. As if he hadn't been holding all the cards....*

Look, *he said,* You're of a certain age. Anyone scanned is going to show something. I know I would. But these indicate damage and each lesion is the evidence.

To me the scars looked like radioactive burns. Something uranium might leave on the skin, so powerful it had seared straight in. But that's a death sentence....

Okay, I'm also starting now to think I'm prone to dizziness. On one of our days at the house I fell asleep and Beppe joked about the heat, saying I wasn't used to it.

Which is true. Anyway, that first day we were late. It had been difficult to reach the house as there were collapsed roads among those hills. It's earthquake country, remember.

All we could hear in the silence were goat bells. I'd glance up from my table under the willow and think, there's nothing here to stop me getting on with… what? Finding the right word? I don't think that would have impressed Ned. But I'd ensured I could write from a table outside. The perfect place for a desk.

Okay, I nodded off and suddenly there was Venus looking over one shoulder and Jupiter over the other. Where had the day gone? Where had all the days gone?

Yes, Beppe's house was like a dream but I swear everything I'm writing down actually happened. On that land is a well with a wooden cover for that well and a bucket on a pulley and the wellwater a long way down like light at a tunnel's end.

To tell the truth I hated travelling through those Italian tunnels when I first drove there and back in the lorry. Subterranean homesick, that was me, sweaty palms on the steering wheel of a big white Iveco.

But somehow we were in the Iveco together, me, Beppe, Ned, the Romanian, all of us. Susan from Palermo was there too, complaining about the marble staircases of another palazzo, taking the bags upstairs, downstairs on those impossible steps. She told us she was born in Kenya and her daughter in Italy. But the girl wanted to speak English. So Susan asked us straight out, could they both come over to…? Did we think…? Was there a chance…?

Took us all by surprise but it's the inevitable question. Why not? we all barked. Of course, I could have told her why not but didn't have the heart. I was too ashamed.

Yes, the bottom of the well or light in the tunnel. And in the distance were the temples at Agrigento. They must be what some of the migrants see when they come north in those boats. There in the mist before dawn are pillars above the beach. Temples that have stood for nearly three thousand years. The first sign of Europe for those travellers.

The best of us, I'd say, those people. Transfixed by the myth of our world of push-button tides and digital air con. By our antihistamine ecology.

But how quickly 'migrant' has become a dirty word. They were gambling everything, trying the old routes, forging new ones. What do we expect? Their phones show them the bounty that might be won. And it's us on those phones. We're making the calls. I promise you those people are coming all the way. We can't stop life.

I blame the sun and another glass of Grillo. Yes, I woke under the willow. Such was breakfast, a blood orange, the chilly white. But don't think I've not seen the malarial babies and the old people with glaucoma. Seen the desperate and the brilliant who brought them. They had been hidden in the backs of Ivecos, then were afloat for days, padlocked into holds. Galley slaves, I tell you, all their money spent on broken down guzzos, on inflatables or any Libyan ketch half trustworthy. Trafficked.

Which is exactly the right word. Like drugs, but we need those drugs. I might have done it myself, driving the lorry back that time from Durazzo, a family hidden in its sleeping compartment. Only I went under the Alps, while they're coming across the Med….

It was me smuggled the child across the Sham desert in that bus out of Baghdad. Or was it our camera, swaddled to protect it from dust? It might easily have been a baby. That Sony travelled on my lap for twenty-four hours and there I sat, smoothing its brow, checking its pulse, staring out at the worst landscape you could imagine. As if the moon was black.

I'd seen our cameraman, doing the same, stroking the Sony and calling it 'my daughter, my daughter….' We'd met his real daughter, aged twelve, standing up in her cot, humming a lullaby. Palsied, the poor kid. When I looked into her eyes I thought I was swimming. Bottomless, those pools….

Yes, I felt giddy. It was Beppe's voice that woke me. But I remember the dream he interrupted. You see, there's a story for everyone. Only we've stopped listening. We can't take it any more. But do you know what it means if you stop listening?

We all warmed to Beppe because he loved that land. It was his family's immemorial land and his grandmother lives there still. But Beppe talked about his home like a man who's returned from a bad place.

So, he cooked for us and told us about the different ricotta, and the pigs he fed on fennel. He promised we would taste the aniseed in his pork. It was that meat he prepared outside after I found enough firewood. It was his own olive oil too and his fennel in the orange salad. All that fennel, that's why the fields were yellow. Those people simply cooked what they grew.

Reading between the lines, Beppe had covered the waterfront. The actual word he used was 'playboy', but I don't think he knew what that implied. So I'm trying to translate. He was speaking English but he tried to explain his own language to us.

We were out in the dusk one night, counting the constellations, a blizzard of moths in the mosquito lamps as we talked. Around here we don't see moths anymore. It's taken me years to notice what's missing now. Which means it's too late....

Anyway, there are two planets together, he told us. For this special occasion. Yes, it's rare, *we said.* Coming together like that. *I didn't ask him which was which. So now I know the central upper Sicilian for 'stars'. Or, I know the sound my mouth should make when I say that word. Kind of humbling. Maybe that's why I was lying down, trying to find the right music for the word. Or perhaps I was looking at the sky.*

Yes, where had all those days gone? At dusk on the last day it was time to light the fire. Beppe was a busy man but when he texted he would be coming home with his own food I found myself nominated to gather firewood. Position of honour, so I listed everything I could find: olive, aloe, prickly pear; kindled with cactus, our firelight on the hill. Sicilian driftwood in the air and snow on Etna still.

Thinking about that town, little Ned ruled the square, serving granita, juggling plates. He even had time to play football with us but it can be hard to get your ball back in that place. Boy, he was being run ragged but always kept a smile on his face. As if he was delighted to be alive. And around him sat the old men in their appointed places, tiny vermilion drinks set before them. Drinks they never touched.

Guess who Ned reminded me of? After it was put together I looked at the statue in a museum in Mazara. Beautiful child, I thought. Sea-faun with bronze braids over a Syrian face. Elf ears too, unmistakable. It was supposed to be a satyr, dancing in bliss. The sculptor had captured the creature in a two-thousand-year-old casting. Being a satyr, there's a considerable Luigi. Fair enough, I thought. And satyrs were not circumcised. But a gorgeous sea-beast, that dancer in a dusty room. Mafioso with alabaster eyes.

After that last meal he cooked for us on the open fire our time was up. We had to leave and I realised we wouldn't be seeing Beppe again. But what he did was to spell out the name of the house where we'd been staying. That house we couldn't explain. 'San Todaro' I think his writing says.

Above all, Beppe was careful to show us the white stone where we should hide the key to the gates when we left for the final time. A stone amongst other stones in the fennel field. And that's the last thing Beppe said to us. When we leave San Todaro, climbing its broken road, to be sure the gates beside the well and the willow are locked. It's the only way to stay safe.

That's it. That's how 'The Satyr' reads, spread over twenty-three Moleskine pages.

But what did some people call the old man? *Taran*, that was it. The god of thunder, a god who could make children cry and grown men duck their heads. Yes, a not inconsiderable god. Forgotten I suppose? As they all must be. But, I tell you, there's more to come. And we have to save what's left.

'Sicilian Driftwood' is from a prose collection about the consequences of climate change and migration in the near future. **Robert Minhinnick**'s novel, *Limestone Man*, reviewed at newwelshreview.com on 1 October, was published in 2015 by Seren. Robert will be reading this story at a benefit, 'Sicilian Driftwood: Readings for Refugees', organised by Sustainable Wales, on Friday, December 11, at 8pm in the Green Room, 5, James St., Porthcawl CF36 3BG, entrance £3, copies of this magazine on sale.

VIOLENCE AND TRANSFORMATION IN PASCALE PETIT'S POETRY

KATRINA NAOMI

Dawn Skorczewski states:

> *Critics of confessional poetry oscillate between celebrating representations of private pain as long-needed and redemptive for society and denigrating or chastising poets who suffered (or cause their readers to suffer) too much.... [T]he critic seems to be in a position to decide how much is too much. Such poetry is often deemed too much when the poet's subject matter is a woman or a child and when the issues are violence, silence and power.*[1]

Violence in the forms of childhood rape and sexual abuse are powerful themes in Pascale Petit's poetry. I focus on the collections *The Zoo Father* (Seren, 2001) and *The Huntress* (Seren, 2005), which respond to Petit's rape by her father and to her mother's mental illness, alongside references to *What the Water Gave Me: Poems After Frida Kahlo* (Seren, 2010).

Her highly personal yet 'fabulatory'[2] poetry has attracted both admirers and detractors. DM Black, writing on *The Zoo Father*'s 'brilliant device' (Petit's use of 'exotic imagery of the Amazon jungle' to discuss what is 'frightening' and 'violent'), 'allows these poems to be truly created objects' (*Poetry London*, no 41, 2002). Others accuse her of being 'garish and indiscreet' (Wayne Burrows, *Poetry London*, no 55, 2006), and Noel Williams finds 'the yoking of beauty and horror... deliberately testing' (*The North*, no 44, 2009). Additional critiques include readers feeling 'bombarded' (Hilary Llewellyn-Williams, *Poetry Wales*, no 38, 2002). Johnny Marsh states regarding *What the Water Gave Me*, 'The constant recurrence of gynaecological and anatomical detail... can become repetitive and too much of an effect' (*Agenda*, no 44, 2009).

I counted the number of uses of the word 'vagina' in *What the Water Gave Me*. Petit mentions the word once, with a mere six references to 'sex', 'hole', 'crotch' and 'pelvis' in fifty-three poems. I wonder if there are topics some critics would prefer (female) poets did not tackle.

Whether or not the 'yoking of beauty and horror' transcends taste depends on the individual. I intend to show that there is far more than a mirroring or reflection of rape and abuse in Petit's poetry. Her imagery, in particular, is highly transformative, even lavish. She renders what could have been a monotony of abuse into vivid poetry, with conflicting emotions shown towards her parents.

'Self-Portrait with Fire Ants' is from *The Zoo Father*:

Self-Portrait with Fire Ants

To visit you Father, I wear a mask of fire ants.
When I sit waiting for you to explain

why you abandoned me when I was eight
they file in, their red bodies

massing around my eyes, stinging my pupils white
until I'm blind. Then they attack my mouth.

I try to lick them but they climb down my gullet
until an entire swarm stings my stomach,

while you must become a giant anteater,
push your long sticky tongue down my throat,

as you once did to my baby brother,
French-kissing him while he pretended to sleep.

I can't remember what you did to me, but the ants know.

For a 'self-portrait' we see very little of the narrator's features. However, her pain is apparent, 'stinging my pupils white / until I'm blind' and 'they [the fire ants] attack my mouth'. The narrator is rendered blind and unable to speak. Dori Laub finds that 'speakers about trauma on some level prefer silence so as to protect themselves from the fear of being listened to – and of listening to themselves'.[3] Petit does find her voice within the poem but the voice does not come easily.

The first three stanzas all have a strong 't' consonant at the end of the first line: 'ants', 'eight', 'white', which softens in the fourth stanza, 'gullet', and is subsumed, as the father transforms, into 'anteater' in the fifth stanza. The strong 't' is reinforced in 'throat'. Once the focus switches to the brother, in the sixth stanza, the 't' disappears, only to return in the final stanza with 'ants'. These uses of 't' produce a stuttering effect in the poem, as though the narrator is struggling to enunciate, the memories and associated emotions of abuse catching in her throat.

The metaphors work on several levels. She cannot speak, and is waiting for her father, 'to explain / why you abandoned me when I was eight.' She is rendered dumb due to his presence and the pain of the memories that meeting him evoke. Further, she becomes blind due to this pain. Is this the pain of seeing him? Or the pain of not having seen him for so many years?[4] Either way, this is the man who abused her (and her brother and mother).

Petit seeks to distance herself from the content via the strategy of masking, yet the mask in this poem is painful – the mask attacks her. The mask could also represent her anger, 'their [the fire ants'] red bodies'. An additional reading of the redness of the 'mask' could be embarrassment and difficulty, her face and body colouring due to seeing her father again. Petit's use of masking is important to her poetry – *The Zoo Father*'s cover image is a horse mask – and masking can be seen throughout *What the Water Gave Me*. Additionally, writing as Frida Kahlo, Petit adopts a persona, another form of mask, in order to explore difficult issues – including Kahlo's crippling accident in a bus crash in which a steel rod pierced her vagina. In 'Remembrance of an Open Wound', Petit likens this piercing to a rape, in which Kahlo loses 'her virginity to a lightning bolt'.

In 'Self-Portrait with Fire Ants', the self-portrait shows what happens inside, where the fire ants 'climb down my gullet / until an entire swarm stings my stomach.' The self-portrait is like an X-ray or ultrasound scan. She shows the effects of the rape inside the body, in addition to the portrayal of her emotions – red face and body, stung by the experience. The internal 'stinging' is visceral: 'the entire swarm' climbs down to sting the reader too.

Elsewhere, her pain is rarely directly shown. She uses metaphor, particularly via masking. Petit does show her loss of control in 'I try to lick them but they climb down my gullet.' This memory of the attack is too strong, something she cannot face, and she writes 'I can't remember' as in cannot or will not remember. She returns again to the relative (if painful) safety of the 'mask', with the final phrase 'but the ants know'; in other words, the mask knows whereas Petit is unable to express what happened.

In this respect it is significant that there are no graphic descriptions of rape in 'Self-Portrait with Fire Ants'. The strongest depictions of rape in *The Zoo Father* are in 'Self-Portrait as a Yanomami Daughter' –

the way you used to hold me, Father,
when you turned into a demon
and tore me with your penis.

This is how Night was made, my thighs sticky with star-blood,

my mouth flooded with moonseeds.

– and in 'Self-Portrait as a Dugout Canoe':

You stood
astride me, struck zigzag blows
with your axe until I was hollow.

Petit's imagery associated with rape is frequently opulent, turning violent material into something beautiful, as in 'sticky with star-blood' and 'flooded with moonseeds'. This opulence, while admittedly being disturbing, is certainly transformative. In the fifth stanza of 'Self-Portrait with Fire Ants', the father shape-shifts, becoming an animal: 'while you must become a giant anteater, / push your long sticky tongue down my throat.' While an anteater can remove some of the pain by eating the ants which bite Petit's 'gullet' and 'stomach', a 'giant anteater' is threatening due to its size. Further, 'push your long sticky tongue down my throat' is a metaphor for forced oral sex. The level of threat is reinforced in the sixth stanza when we are told the father pushed his tongue into the narrator's brother's mouth, 'French-kissing him while he pretended to sleep.' Ignoring the play on words of 'French-kissing', given that Petit's mother and father were French, we realise that the father is a serial abuser.

The father's transformation into animal form, using magic realism and Petit's highly stylised imagery, represents an innovative way of writing about pain and sexual abuse in contemporary poetry. Furthermore, as Gregson points out, by using various animals to represent her father, Petit is satirising

> *masculine appetites, especially sexual appetites. Patriarchal assumptions insist that the masculine is rational and therefore properly human, whereas the feminine is irrational and so related to nature in all its disorder.*[6]

In *The Zoo Father*, such assumptions are turned on their head, with the father frequently appearing to be irrational and 'beastly'.

'Self-Portrait with Fire Ants' contains six uses of 'you' (and one use of 'your'), something which paradoxically might be expected in a love poem and is reminiscent of Sylvia Plath's 'Daddy'[7] (although Petit's uses of 'you' are less emphatic). Compulsion features in the poem, as in 'while you must become a giant anteater'. That word 'must' appears frequently in Petit's poetry, and could be seen as symptomatic of how she was forced against her will.

The use of couplets for such a poem conveys subliminally the notion of a 'coupling'. Gregson, in an uncomfortable, yet nuanced, reading of *The Zoo Father*, points to an uneasy reciprocity in the daughter–father relationship, particularly in 'Self-Portrait as a Harpy Eagle'.[8]

A highly problematic parental relationship can also be sensed in Petit's poetry about her mother. 'My Mother's Tongue', from *The Huntress*, picks up on some of Petit's key themes – power, silence and violence. Writing without stanza breaks (as in much of *The Huntress*), she heightens the intensity of the poems, allowing the reader no breathing space.

My Mother's Tongue

I have twisted a lightning bolt
into a spiral and eaten it.
From my stomach it gives orders.
I, who was never hugged by you,
or hugged you, Mother,
must lie on your corpse
feet to feet, breasts to breasts,
mouth to mouth.
I cannot help the words I am speaking
but say them without pause
in the language of your 'angel'.
I give you my body to eat,
my blood to drink,
my flesh for clothes.
I give you my breath.
You struggle and I wrestle with you
as you rise from the floor.
Now your black and shrivelled tongue
is hanging out of your mouth
and I must seize it and tear it out.
Then you fall down. The door opens.
And I leave, holding your tongue
in my cupped hands like a bird
that must be saved,
its wing-bones and spine
curved like an embryo.
I go out into the great field
and set it free.

As with almost any Petit poem, imagery dominates. Here, Roman Catholic imagery prevails, with suggestions of transubstantiation: 'I give you my body to eat, / my blood to drink.' Continuing with religious imagery, there is an 'angel' and a reference to speaking in tongues: 'I cannot help the words I am speaking / but say them without pause / in the language of your "angel".'

In contrast to 'Self-Portrait with Fire Ants', where the narrator is 'dumb', here she speaks freely but 'cannot help' what she is saying, or doing. There is no guilt, she has the 'angel' on her side. In addition, the 'lightning bolt'[9] 'gives orders', telling the narrator what she must do. She has to lie on her mother's dead body: 'must lie on your corpse / feet to feet, breasts to breasts, / mouth to mouth'. In addition to the suggestion of being controlled, there is a bodily sacrifice, with the daughter 'who was never hugged by you, / or hugged you, Mother,' offering herself for consumption – her body to eat, her blood to drink – as in the Roman Catholic mass. However, this is female blood, which many associate with shamanistic and other transformative powers. She also offers her mother 'my flesh for clothes' and her own 'breath', continuing this sacrifice in a bid to cover the mother's nakedness and resuscitate, or save and protect her. The violent religious imagery continues with the metaphor of wrestling with an angel: 'You struggle and I wrestle with you / as you rise from the floor.'

The poem becomes far more violent from line 18. We hear of the mother's 'black and shrivelled tongue' which Petit 'must seize' and 'tear... out'. As well as a silencing, which is suggestive of how Petit was silenced as a child, this could reference the rape of Philomela by Tereus in Ovid's *Metamorphoses*. Line 23 has the revelation of Petit saving her mother's tongue 'in my cupped hands like a bird', with the tongue's 'wing-bones and spine / curved like an embryo', as if Petit offers her mother's tongue, and her stories, a new life. Like Sharon Olds in 'I Go Back to May 1937' (*The Gold Cell*), Petit liberates what happens to her mother, and by inference what she has personally experienced: 'I go out into the great field

/ and set it free', the 'great field' being outdoors, away from secrecy and silence.

Petit uses linked internal rhymes and half-rhymes of 'spiral' and 'angel', 'struggle' and 'wrestle' and 'shrivelled' and 'fall' and 'field', which bring a sense of returning to what has gone before. Each rhyme links the mother and the daughter, possibly signifying that, as her mother was raped, so Petit was raped. Despite the violent imagery and content, the poem can be seen as a love poem to her mother, offering her rebirth and freedom, while the poet also seizes the chance for her own freedoms.

As we have seen, tongues and mouths appear frequently in Petit's work, as in 'Self-Portrait with Fire Ants', alluding to silence and the breaking of that silence. Another poem in *The Huntress*, 'House of Darkness', ends with 'a blade / called the Perforator / "for piercing the tongues of daughters who talk".'

Daughters who talk too much can be criticised. Robert Potts accuses Petit of 'therapy' in his review of *The Zoo Father*, claiming 'poets who take suffering as subject matter do so knowing the risks.' He does not explain what the risks might be, yet continues:

> *It is hard to criticise material so apparently personal.... The subject matter has its own power; does the poetry transform it sufficiently from any other account of appalling abuse? Not entirely, not sufficiently. The same poetic procedure is applied in nearly every poem, the same drama of childhood impotence converted into adult omnipotence through acts of imagination. There could have been one, perhaps two powerful poems to be extracted from this approach.*

He concludes: 'At book length, *The Zoo Father* asks that we participate in the gruelling experience of someone else's therapy.'[10] His assertion that poems in *The Zoo Father* all take the same 'approach' shows a casual reading of the collection. Not all the poems are hostile to the father. Some, such as 'The Lungfish Father', are far removed from violence, appearing to show Petit's desire to help her father breathe:

> *I'd secrete bubbles of oxygen*
> *from my blood*
> *and waft them over your mouth.*

In contrast to the emotions shown in 'The Lungfish Father', see the energy and transformation of the self in 'Amazonia':

> *I'm hallucinating as any true*
> *hunter should, having fasted and lain here awake, chanting*
> *to the spirits on the ceiling. This is how I make paint*
> *ripple into a white forest canopy, the trees burst into flower*
> *and flowers turn into monkeys.*

Further, 'The Songs of Insects' contains lyrical lines such as, 'If moonlight could be heard / it would sound like this.'

While there is a good deal of violence in *The Zoo Father*, the tone of the collection is far more varied than critics have allowed. In my interview with her,[11] Petit spoke of wanting to exhibit both anger and compassion, the good and the bad, in her poetry:

> *I am acting out a kind of struggle. I'm looking at evil… and I'm looking at where the goodness is… but at the same time I really acknowledge there's a lot of darkness there, there's a lot of violence.*

The emotions in her work are complex and her imagery is often opulent and frequently troubling. The representations of her father and mother are nuanced, at times even loving. This represents a duality to her work, highlighting her conflicting emotions and subtly subverting gender expectations. In doing so, and in moving beyond passivity or a 'victim' role, Petit's poetry has opened up innovative channels of writing in response to sexual violence, ones which do not always tackle rape directly but which shed fresh light on transformative life experiences.

Katrina Naomi's second full poetry collection, *The Way the Crocodile Taught Me*, will be published by Seren in April. Her latest pamphlet is *Hooligans* (Rack Press), inspired by the suffragettes. She recently completed a PhD in creative writing at Goldsmiths.

Poems published in full with kind permission of Pascale Petit.

Footnotes:

[1] Dawn Skorczewski, 'Whose Prison is This? Literary Critics Cover Incest in Anne Sexton's "Briar Rose"', *Signs*, 21.2 (Winter 1966), 309-42 (p 309), cited in Meryl Pugh, 'Someone Else's Therapy?: Reading *The Zoo Father*' (unpublished, Goldsmiths, 2008). I am indebted to Pugh for sharing her essay with me.

[2] Ian Gregson, *The New Poetry in Wales* (Cardiff: University of Wales Press, 2007), p 117.

[3] Dori Laub, 'Bearing Witness or the Vicissitudes of Listening', in *Testimony: Crises of Witnessing in Literature, Psychoanalysis and History*, eds Shoshana Felman and Dori Laub (London: Routledge, 1992), http://representingtheholocaust.wikispaces.com/file/view/Laub_Bearing+Witness.pdf

[4] In subsequent poems such as 'The Lungfish Father', we realise the father is seriously ill.

[5] 'Self-Portrait as a Were-Jaguar', in *The Zoo Father*, refers to Petit's father's rape of her mother, while 'Self-Portrait with Fire Ants' refers to Petit's brother's abuse.

[6] Gregson, p 119.

[7] Although Petit believes Plath's 'Daddy' has not been an influence. Pascale Petit, private communication to Katrina Naomi, email dated 3 March 2011.

[8] Gregson, p 120.

[9] See the earlier reference to 'lightning bolt'. Both examples suggest the use of force.

[10] Robert Potts, *The Zoo Father*, by Pascale Petit', *Guardian Saturday Review* (16 March 2002). I thank Meryl Pugh for drawing my attention to Potts' review.

[11] My interview with Petit was first published in *Orbis*, no 55, 2011.

> There I was, a homing bird, trying to find a way back, but betraying Home – word by (cooing) word, by writing in English

ON WRITING *PIGEON*

ALYS CONRAN

'LOOK UP PIGEON IN YOUR GOOD FIELD GUIDE, IF YOU HAVE ONE,' SAYS Simon Barnes in *The Bad Birdwatcher's Companion*. 'You will probably find that the pigeon does not exist.' I felt that about many of the children I knew growing up. Their stories pecked around in the background, unheard. The child whose mother left his hair uncombed every time after the nit treatment, little black bugs paralysed in his mousy locks. The girl who regularly had cigarette burns on her china-white hands. The faltering teenager who told what was done to her at youth club, and was disbelieved. There are a lot of pigeons in Wales.

In my twenties, moving my temporary bird box of a life between cities in the UK and abroad, where a nice unobtrusive dash of ethnicity was for the most part a badge of honour in artistic and creative circles, I felt a bit of a pigeon too. And it was 'as if pigeons were an embarrassment to birdwatchers – as if pigeons were an embarrassment to proper birds,' because Welshness, especially the liminal, obtrusive, politically urgent blend of it I'm made of, didn't seem quite appropriate.

But, as the bad birdwatcher puts it, 'Pigeons, however, exist.... Try telling them they're not proper birds.' And so, in my shy young adulthood, the pigeon in me shimmered greyly, its feathers tinged with green and purple, like slate.

The pigeon my book's named for is a young boy, shoulders delicate as eggshells. Almost as soon as I started writing he wandered across the page in a vagabond, alternately lively and listless way, and he caused trouble always, sticking strawberry chewing gum to the high, white ceiling of my flat on Meadow Place in Edinburgh, or scratching his name onto the perspex window of Barcelona's Línia 4 Metro carriage as I made my way home from work. I didn't find a place to put him for ages. But he was a genie not happy to wander his way back into his pigeonhole, so he eventually trespassed onto some uncategorised pages of writing, made friends with a haunted young girl called Iola, who competed despite herself for the role of protagonist, and made a novel that's both a battleground and a love story. Iola has a great love for Pigeon. When I think of him, I ache.

When I think of my novel with his name, I cower. It's been a painful process. *Pigeon* was born of the conflict between the language of my pen and its subject – the Welsh heartland I was writing myself back to. The book wouldn't exist without that essential untranslated heart and the related guilt which bleeds across its pages. There I was, a homing bird, trying to find a way back, but betraying Home – word by (cooing) word, by writing in English.

Still, the peopled landscape of my book spoke insistently, in unbordered Welsh and English, and I caught at the words, like catching snowflakes. And if I betrayed Pigeon by donning English binoculars, the guilt about that was galvanising. Perhaps I wouldn't have studied him with the doggedness necessary for his little feet to leave their snowmelt imprint on this book without the guilt mechanism of the linguistic lens I chose.

The story sounds in two voices. One is Iola's first person, and the second is almost, but not quite Pigeon's, the closest I could get to him. To be more intimate, to take on an 'I' would have been an act of ventriloquism he would just spit at. So Pigeon is a 'he' not an 'I', though Iola, says 'I' insistently, without a clue what she means.

The novel, for a long time, was hampered by a fear of Home. I flung all kinds of other places at it, tried to get Pigeon to squat in Barcelona, to wander the hooting streets of Manchester beside me, but he kept flying back to the slate hillside where I now, finally, had set up my own dovecote.

Pigeon made me write a novel that isn't in Welsh, and also isn't quite in English, and he filled it with the kind of story I felt unable to write without him, in which such grand things as murders and miscarriages of justice happen. Which they do, especially to pigeons, and especially here.

Unlike me, Pigeon's a fearless storyteller, incisive, spirited, occasionally cruel. In this novel he suffers the consequences of his own story-making, is labelled as both a criminal pest (pigeon) and a powerless innocent (dove), has his wings clipped, loses his mate at least for a while, loses and then tries to regain his song, and falls headlong from the sky many times. Like I said, it's been a painful process. But this whole pidgin book happened so that he might be witnessed through more than just binoculars, and so the green and purple sheen of his feathers might startle, as he skulks along these up and down slate streets carrying our unsilent messages. Lively. Resilient. And still a homing bird.

Alys Conran's fiction, poetry, and translations have been placed in several competitions, including the Bristol Short Story Prize and the Manchester Fiction Prize. Her work is to be found in magazines and anthologies, most recently *Stand* and *The Manchester Review*. She completed her MA in Creative Writing at Manchester, drafting *Pigeon*, her first novel, while she was there, and completing it while she ran projects to increase access to creative writing and reading among traditionally excluded groups in north Wales. She was recently awarded a scholarship to write a second novel as part of a PhD at Bangor, where she also teaches. *Pigeon*, a novel about secrets, and about the challenges and survival of childhood friendship, will be published by Parthian in May.

Don't miss

NEW WELSH READER

CREATIVE & ESSAYS (Summer 2016):

Power in the Land? Wylfa, Nuclear Power, Landscape & Art:
Essays, poetry and criticism curated by Philippa Holloway
Stories by Francesca Rhydderch, Alex Barr, Marie Darrieussecq & Jon Harrison

NEW WELSH REVIEW

REVIEWS, OPINION & MULTIMEDIA:

Clown's Shoes, Rebecca F John (audio review)
Video interview: Tony Bianchi (*Harry Selwyn's Last Race*)
The Man at the Corner Table, Rosie Shepperd (audio review)
Poetry showcase video: Alys Conran, Claire Booker, Stav Poleg & Polly Atkin
Over the Line, An Introduction to Poetry Comics, eds Chrissy Williams & Tom Humberstone (text review)

NEW WELSH RAREBYTE

Amazon Kindle ebook out now

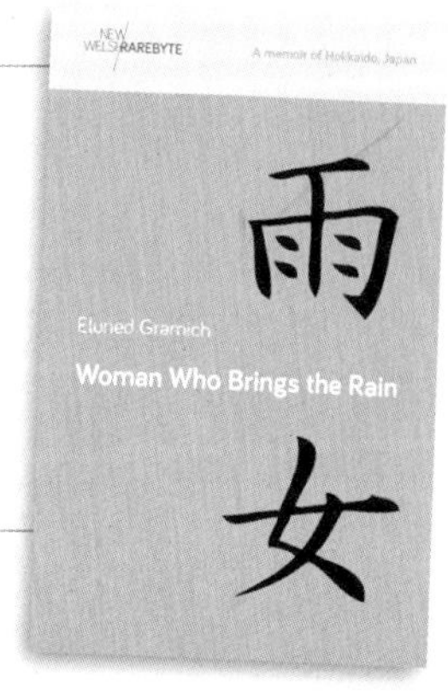